BEGINNING PROMPT ENGINEERING

Learning to communicate with
Large Language Models

Chris Jordan OE BEng(Hons
Extended)

I dedicate this volume to my father.

*George Frankham Jordan lived a full and adventurous life that
was cut short far too soon.*

*Its only now as I get older I realise how much of the adventure he
was still living. Age doesn't define us and our time on this world
doesnt either. It really is what we do and what we leave behind.*

CONTENTS

Title Page

Copyright

Dedication

Introduction   1

Unravelling the Mysteries of Prompt Engineering   3

The Prompt Engineer's Tool Kit: Essential Skills   9

Secrets of the Trade: Prompt Engineering Techniques   66

Case Studies in Prompt Engineering   105

The Future of Prompt Engineering   116

Beyond The Web Interface: Diverse Applications of Prompts 129

Embarking on Your Prompt Engineering Journey: Next   140
Steps

Conclusion: Embracing the Loom of the Future   145

INTRODUCTION

Welcome aboard this exciting journey into the fascinating world of prompt engineering. If you're looking to uncover the mysteries surrounding this field, or if you've ever wondered how language models interact so cleverly with us humans, you've picked up the right guide.

In the rapidly evolving landscape of artificial intelligence, the role of prompt engineering stands out as a key player. It's the secret ingredient that empowers AI language models to understand and respond to our queries. And yet, it remains an enigma to most. But worry not! This book is here to pull back the curtain.

Designed for beginners, this book introduces you to the core concepts, techniques, and applications of prompt engineering in an engaging, informative, and fun manner. You'll learn about the intriguing science behind AI language models, the essential skills for a prompt engineer, and the magic you can create with well-crafted prompts.

We'll start with the basics, using everyday experiences and memorable metaphors to make complex ideas more accessible. We'll then delve into examples of real-world uses of prompt engineering, showcasing both the victories and the ouch moments. We'll also cast an eye towards the future, exploring upcoming trends and the ethical considerations shaping this field.

What this book is not, is a dense textbook filled with jargon and complicated algorithms. Instead, we've strived to keep the material light, engaging, and informative. We want you to enjoy the learning process, and leave with a firm grasp of the topic, and more importantly, the curiosity and confidence to explore further.

By the end of this book, you will not only understand what prompt engineering is, but you will also have a clearer picture of how you can leverage these skills, whether you're considering a career in this burgeoning field, or simply fascinated by the potential of AI.

We hope that this will be the first of many steps you take into the world of prompt engineering and that this book sparks a deep and enduring interest in AI and its infinite possibilities. Welcome to your new superhero career. Let the journey begin!

UNRAVELLING THE MYSTERIES OF PROMPT ENGINEERING

Welcome to the start of a thrilling voyage into the world of prompt engineering, where the mystique of technology meets the charm of language, and where human ingenuity fuels the magic of artificial intelligence. If you've ever marvelled at your smartphone's knack for witty comebacks or gasped as your virtual assistant pulled a surprisingly profound piece of advice seemingly out of thin air, then you've already had a sneak peek at the wonders of prompt engineering. But, as you'll soon find out, this was just the tip of the iceberg.

This chapter peels back the layers of this intriguing discipline, making it more approachable and less of an enigma. From the captivating narrative of its rise and relevance to the 'abracadabra' behind AI language models, and onto the exhilarating job role of a prompt engineer.

The Enigma That Is Prompt Engineering: An Exciting Story

Imagine a world brimming with conversations—chitter-chatter that fills the air in crowded city squares, the silent dialogue between a novelist and their word processor, the digital banter that flits across cyberspace in the form of tweets, texts, and comments. Now, envision a special breed of engineers who have found a way to navigate this seemingly chaotic sea of words, gleaning context, extracting meaning, and sparking responsive dialogues. These are the prompt engineers, the puppeteers who guide artificial intelligence in the grand theatre of human communication.

At its core, prompt engineering is about turning jumbled symbols into human-like conversation. It's about orchestrating a harmonious dance between human curiosity and machine intelligence, guiding the latter to respond with wit, wisdom, or just the right information. But where did it all start? And how did it evolve into an integral part of the AI we see today?

The journey of prompt engineering begins with the advent of computer programming, where commands were carefully crafted to extract specific outcomes from a machine. But as computers became more sophisticated and the demands on their capabilities grew, we soon realized that teaching machines to understand and respond to natural human language was a monumental task. It was a quest to impart the nuance, the cultural context, the idioms, and the sheer unpredictability of human conversation into a being of silicon and code.

The rise of machine learning and AI offered new opportunities to push the boundaries. The development of language models, like the renowned GPT series by OpenAI, marked a significant milestone. Suddenly, we had algorithms that could generate human-like text that was not just grammatically correct, but also contextually relevant and shockingly creative.

Yet, these models didn't achieve their finesse by accident. Behind every sharp AI response, there was a meticulously crafted prompt

—designed and refined by the unseen hands of prompt engineers.

Today, prompt engineering is not just an interesting anecdote in the story of AI—it's a crucial discipline shaping our digital interactions. Every time you ask Siri about the weather or Google Assistant about the latest football scores, a prompt engineer's craft comes into play. When businesses deploy chatbots to handle customer queries, or when researchers use AI to sift through mountains of data, the value of effective prompts becomes evident.

The enigma of prompt engineering lies not only in the technical complexity but also in the marvel of human creativity and linguistic understanding required to shape effective prompts.

As we delve deeper into this engaging story, remember that every great prompt engineer started where you are right now—with curiosity, excitement, and perhaps, just a touch of apprehension. So, ready to uncover the exciting narrative behind prompt engineering? The stage is set, the curtain lifts, and your adventure begins!

The Magic Behind Ai-Language Models: A Simple Breakdown

Have you ever watched a magician pull a rabbit out of a hat and wondered, "How on earth did they do that?" Watching the way an AI language model works can bring on a similar sense of disbelief. How did it do that? One moment, you feed it a simple prompt—a question, a statement, a piece of code—and the next moment, it responds with information, a joke, or even an entire short story. This rabbit-out-of-a-hat trick might seem like magic, but the real magic lies in the blend of sophisticated technology and clever engineering.

Let's break it down. AI language models, like OpenAI's GPT series, are trained on an enormous amount of text data—from books, articles, and websites, to conversations, scripts, and everything in between. Picture this training process as teaching a child to speak but on a much grander scale. Just as a child learns language by listening to the people around them, an AI model learns from the data it's fed.

But how do prompts come into play?

Think of prompts as a compass guiding a ship through the vast ocean of language. They provide the direction for our AI, pointing it towards the kind of response we seek. For instance, if you ask the model, "What's the weather like today?", the AI, powered by prompt engineering, doesn't just see it as a string of words. Instead, it deciphers the context, the intent behind the question— you want to know about today's weather conditions—and crafts a suitable response.

AI language models achieve this feat through something called "transformer architecture", a nifty piece of tech that allows them to consider the entire context of a given input when generating a response. It's like having a bird's-eye view of a maze, enabling the AI to chart the best course towards the correct response.

But the brilliance of these models lies not just in their understanding of language, but also in their creativity. Feed it the start of a fairy tale, and it could spin you a story complete with plot twists and charming characters. Challenge it with a coding problem, and it might provide a solution that would make even seasoned programmers nod in approval.

The fascinating part is that all this magic—every nuanced response, every amusing anecdote, every insightful fact—comes from a series of mathematical calculations guided by the prompt. The model assigns probabilities to potential next words, based on its training, and generates responses that match the highest probabilities given the context.

It's important to remember, though, that while AI language models might seem magical, they're not infallible. They can sometimes produce incorrect or nonsensical responses. They might not understand sarcasm, humour, or cultural nuances as well as a human does. But that's where the true artistry of a prompt engineer comes in—crafting prompts that bring out the best in the model and mitigate its limitations.

So, as we dive deeper into the magic of prompt engineering, remember: you're not just learning to control an AI model. You're learning to harness a formidable force of mathematical wizardry, using prompts as your wand. In this world, the perfect prompt can truly make a world of difference. Let's continue our journey and discover how to craft those perfect prompts in the exciting role of a prompt engineer.

Don The Cape, Be The Prompt Engineer: Your New Superhero Career

Alright, it's time to swap your everyday attire for a superhero cape. Welcome to the world of prompt engineering, where your power is to breathe intelligence into AI, one prompt at a time. But what does this superhero career actually entail? What challenges will you face, and what opportunities lie ahead?

Picture the job of a prompt engineer as being the translator and guide for an eager-to-learn, always-listening AI language model. On one hand, you have humans with their dynamic, diverse, and often chaotic way of expressing ideas. On the other hand, you have an AI model, hungry for precise guidance to understand and respond to these expressions.

In between these two forces, you stand, the prompt engineer, translating human intent into a language the AI can understand and respond to effectively. You craft clever prompts that guide the model, helping it navigate the intricate maze of human language. Your toolbox? A potent mix of linguistic understanding, creativity, and a keen grasp of the model's strengths and weaknesses.

You're also a detective of sorts, always learning and adapting. You test different prompts, analyze how the model responds, and adjust your strategies. No two days are the same in this dynamic landscape. One day, you might be refining prompts for a customer service chatbot. The next day, you could be crafting prompts that help an AI summarize complex medical literature.

But the thrill of prompt engineering doesn't stop at shaping AI interactions. As a prompt engineer, you're a trailblazer in an emerging field. The work you do today could shape how millions, even billions, interact with AI tomorrow. You're also part of a community, a fellowship of like-minded engineers continually learning from and inspiring each other.

Beyond all the technicalities and challenges, being a prompt engineer is about fostering meaningful connections between humans and AI. It's about envisioning a world where AI understands us better, helps us more effectively, and even amuses us from time to time. And in this quest, you're the superhero, the prompt engineer with the power to make AI not just smart, but also relatable, useful, and fun.

So, don your cape and get ready to fly into this exciting new career. Remember, every superhero's journey begins with a single step— or in this case, a single prompt. Let's take that step together and unravel the art and science of prompt engineering.

THE PROMPT ENGINEER'S TOOL KIT: ESSENTIAL SKILLS

Welcome to the heart of our journey, where we unpack the secret weapons of every successful prompt engineer. Here, we venture beyond the surface, diving into the nuts and bolts, the technical know-how that distinguishes a prompt engineer from an average AI enthusiast.

However, don't be daunted by the mention of cryptic codes, machine learning jargon, or data interpretation. In this part of our guide, we will approach these topics with the same flair and whimsy that we've journeyed with so far. The aim isn't to turn you into a data scientist overnight, but rather, to provide you with the essential skills and understanding that will empower you as a prompt engineer.

From a friendly introduction to AI and machine learning to a fun exploration of Python (the prompt engineer's lingua franca), and a dive into the intriguing world of Natural Language Processing, we've got a lot to cover. We'll also delve into the importance of data analysis and interpretation—skills that act as a crystal ball, enabling you to foresee how your prompts will guide the AI.

So, strap in for an exciting journey into the toolkit of a prompt engineer. Don't worry—we've packed this section full of engaging examples, memorable metaphors, and interesting insights to keep things lively and enjoyable. Let's open the toolbox and explore the gear inside!

Ai, Machine Learning And You: A Friendly Introduction

Once upon a time, the idea of creating machines that could think, learn, and understand was the stuff of science fiction. But today, it's not just reality—it's the exciting field of Artificial Intelligence (AI). AI is about engineering the magic of human intelligence into machines.

Now, let's meet the wizard in this magical realm: Machine Learning (ML). ML is a subset of AI that gives machines the ability to learn without being explicitly programmed. It learns and makes decisions based on data to make predictions or decisions without being specifically programmed to perform the task.

One fun example of ML is the recommendation algorithm on your favourite streaming platform. Ever wondered how it seems to know just what movie you're in the mood for? That's ML at work! It learns from your past viewing history, your preferences, and the preferences of viewers with similar tastes. In fact, every time you like a movie or skip a song, you're providing data that helps the ML model learn and improve.

At its core, ML involves training models using large sets of data. This is similar to how you might train a dog to sit by rewarding it with treats. Given enough examples (or treats), the model (or dog) can learn the desired behaviour.

But here's where it gets really exciting: ML is also the backbone of AI language models—the very models that power prompt engineering! Understanding AI and ML provides you with insights into how these models learn and respond to prompts. It's like having a backstage pass to the greatest show in tech!

So, buckle up and get ready for an enchanting journey into the world of AI and ML. By the end of this friendly introduction, you'll feel at home with terms like 'neural networks', 'supervised learning', 'unsupervised learning', and 'reinforcement learning'. And most importantly, you'll have taken the first major step in your prompt engineering journey—understanding the very foundation on which this field is built!

We'll start by pulling the cloak off the elusive term 'neural networks'. You've probably heard of the term, and maybe even used it in a conversation. But what exactly is a neural network? It's an algorithmic construct that imitates the human brain, aiming to make decisions in a similar way to how we humans do. Composed of interconnected 'neurons' or nodes, it takes in inputs, processes them through hidden layers using weights that are adjusted during training, and finally, produces an output.

Just like a child learns to identify a dog by associating certain features like four legs, tail, fur, etc., a neural network learns to make predictions by fine-tuning its weights based on the inputs it receives and the errors in its predictions. It's through this iterative process of trial and error that the neural network becomes smarter.

Next up, we have three main categories of machine learning: supervised learning, unsupervised learning, and reinforcement learning. Let's delve into each one.

Supervised learning is the most common type of machine learning, where we have input variables (features) and an output variable (label), and we use an algorithm to learn the mapping function from the input to the output. Think of it as a teacher supervising the learning process. We know the correct answers, and the algorithm iteratively makes predictions on the training data and is corrected by the teacher.

Unsupervised learning, on the other hand, is a type of machine learning where we only have input data and no corresponding output variables. The algorithm is left on its own to discover and present an interesting structure in the data. Imagine you are given a pile of assorted Lego blocks. Without any instructions, you're free to explore, categorize, and construct whatever you like. That's unsupervised learning in a nutshell.

Lastly, reinforcement learning is a type of machine learning where an agent learns how to behave in an environment, by performing certain actions and receiving rewards or penalties in return. Think of it as training a dog - if it behaves well, it gets a treat (positive reinforcement), and if it misbehaves, it might get a time-out (negative reinforcement).

Now, how does all of this fit into the world of prompt engineering? The truth is, every time you interact with an AI language model, you're engaging with the product of these principles. The model has been trained on vast amounts of text data, learned to predict the next word in a sentence, and refined its predictions based on the rewards (correct predictions) and penalties (incorrect predictions) it received during training. It's like a highly advanced form of the classic game of 'fill in the blanks'.

By understanding these fundamentals, you're laying a strong foundation for your prompt engineering journey. But remember, the magic isn't just in understanding, but also in doing. So, roll up your sleeves and get ready to engineer some prompts!

Python And Other Cryptic Codes: The Language Of The Prompt Engineers

Imagine you've just discovered an ancient treasure map, but it's written in a language you can't understand. Without the key to deciphering the symbols, your journey to the treasure is halted. In the world of AI and prompt engineering, that key is Python.

Why Python?

The question isn't so much "Why Python?" as it is "Why not Python?" In the world of prompt engineering and AI, Python has made itself indispensable. Just like English is considered the lingua franca of the world, Python could be considered the lingua franca of AI.

The simplicity of Python is its most charming quality. It's an incredibly readable language, with a clean syntax that's easy to learn and understand. It's like the friendly neighbourhood language that welcomes everyone, regardless of their coding expertise. It's because of this characteristic that Python has often been the first choice for beginners in programming.

Beyond its simplicity, Python's versatility is its another significant strength. It's not just a snake in the grass; it's a powerful beast that can handle a wide array of tasks. From web development to data analysis, machine learning, and much more —Python's got it all covered.

But Python's appeal to prompt engineers specifically lies in its extensive ecosystem of libraries and frameworks. Libraries like NumPy and pandas make data manipulation a breeze, while TensorFlow and PyTorch offer high-level APIs for creating and training complex machine-learning models. And let's not forget about NLTK and spaCy for natural language processing tasks.

In the realm of AI, these libraries are like the magical artefacts that make Python such a powerful ally. Without them, Python would still be a good language, but with them, it becomes the perfect tool for the work of a prompt engineer.

Python 101 - The Basics

Python, like any language, has its own unique set of vocabulary and grammar rules. These constitute the "basics" of Python—the foundational knowledge upon which you'll build as you explore more complex concepts. In this section, we will gently introduce these basics, aiming to make you feel comfortable and confident as you begin to speak Python.

Syntax and Variables

Syntax is the set of rules that defines how programs in Python are written and interpreted. The syntax in Python is designed to be easy to read and write, promoting clean and clear code. One aspect of Python's syntax is the use of variables. Variables in Python are like containers, they hold data and their values can be changed and manipulated. For example, a = 5 here, a is a variable holding the value 5.

Data Types

Python supports a range of data types. Some of the most common ones include integers, floating-point numbers, strings, and Booleans. Each data type has specific characteristics and uses, and knowing which one to use is a crucial part of coding in Python. For example, you'd use a string to store text data and an integer to store whole numbers.

Basic Operations

Python supports a wide array of operations, including mathematical operations, string operations, and logical operations. Mathematical operations are just as you'd expect— addition, subtraction, multiplication, and division—while string operations allow you to manipulate text data. Logical operations, on the other hand, let you make comparisons and test conditions.

Control Flow Statements

These are the building blocks that allow Python (and indeed, all programming languages) to make decisions and repeat tasks.

They include if statements for decision-making and for and while loops for repeated tasks.

Functions

Functions in Python are blocks of reusable code that perform specific tasks. You can think of them as little self-contained programs that you can call upon to help out with your tasks.

Lists, Dictionaries, and Other Data Structures

Python provides several data structures that help us store and manipulate data effectively. These include lists (ordered collections of items), dictionaries (unordered collections of key-value pairs), sets (unordered collections of unique elements), and tuples (ordered, immutable collections of items). Understanding these data structures will allow you to organize and manipulate data in Python effectively.

Error Handling

When you're programming, you're bound to run into errors and exceptions. Python provides mechanisms for handling these errors gracefully, allowing your program to recover from unexpected situations. Learning about try, except, and finally statements will help you write robust and reliable Python code.

Modules and Libraries

Python's power comes from its vast ecosystem of modules and libraries—pre-written pieces of code that provide functionalities to perform many tasks. Python's standard library, for example, includes modules for file I/O, system calls, dates and times, and more. Additionally, there are countless third-party libraries for nearly every use case you can imagine. In this section, we will introduce the concept of modules and libraries and discuss some of the most important ones for prompt engineering, such as

NumPy, pandas, and TensorFlow.

Remember, the aim here is not to make you a Python expert overnight—rather, it's to familiarize you with the language and make it feel less foreign. As you grow more comfortable with these basics, you'll be well-prepared to explore more advanced Python concepts, such as libraries and frameworks that are essential for AI and prompt engineering.

Python Libraries for AI and Prompt Engineering

An essential part of Python's charm lies in its abundant libraries, especially those related to data science, AI, and ML. If you think of Python as a language, then its libraries are like the various dialects, each offering unique ways to express and solve problems. Here's a quick introduction to some of the essential libraries in AI and prompt engineering:

NumPy

Short for Numerical Python, NumPy is a powerful library for numerical computing. It provides support for arrays (multi-dimensional) and matrices, along with a collection of mathematical functions to operate on these data structures.

Pandas

This is the go-to library for anything related to data manipulation and analysis. Whether you're dealing with missing values, merging datasets, or analyzing time series data, pandas have got you covered.

Matplotlib/Seaborn

These libraries are all about data visualization. Matplotlib is a versatile library capable of creating static, animated, and interactive visualizations in Python. Seaborn is built on top of Matplotlib and allows you to create more attractive and informative statistical graphics.

Scikit-learn

When it comes to machine learning, scikit-learn is one of the first libraries that comes to mind. It offers simple and efficient tools for data mining and analysis, and it's built on NumPy, SciPy, and Matplotlib.

TensorFlow and PyTorch

These two are the most widely used libraries in deep learning. They offer flexible platforms for building and training neural networks, and they both have large, supportive communities.

NLTK, spaCy, and Gensim

These libraries are specific to the field of Natural Language Processing (NLP), which lies at the heart of prompt engineering. NLTK (Natural Language Toolkit) is perfect for linguistic data exploration. spaCy is great for tasks requiring deep learning, and Gensim is designed for topic modelling and document similarity analysis.

Let's delve into some of these libraries, showcasing how they are employed in AI and prompt engineering. Remember, though, as important as it is to know these tools, the real art lies in knowing how and when to use them to create your symphony in AI.

NumPy: The Powerhouse of Numerical Computing

NumPy, short for Numerical Python, is the foundational package for mathematical computing in Python. As a prompt engineer, you'll find yourself using NumPy extensively, as it's highly efficient and flexible when it comes to numerical operations.

Imagine NumPy as the powerful engine beneath the hood of your car. While you might not interact with it directly in your day-to-day driving, it's continuously working, ensuring everything runs smoothly. Similarly, NumPy, with its support for high-performance multi-dimensional arrays and matrices, powers much of the data processing in AI.

Its features include:

- A powerful N-dimensional array object
- Sophisticated (broadcasting) functions
- Tools for integrating C/C++ and Fortran code
- Useful linear algebra, Fourier transform, and random number capabilities

The core functionality of NumPy is its ndarray (n-dimensional array) object, which is a fast, flexible container for large datasets in Python. Arrays allow you to perform mathematical operations on whole blocks of data, a feature that comes in handy when you're manipulating large datasets, which is common in AI applications.

Furthermore, libraries like pandas, Matplotlib, and scikit-learn are built on NumPy, using its array data structure and mathematical functions. That makes NumPy a critical tool in your prompt engineering toolkit.

For more on NumPy and its capabilities, you can visit their official documentation at
https://numpy.org/doc/stable/
or check out the code and examples on their GitHub page at
https://github.com/numpy/numpy

Remember, the path to mastering NumPy is through practice, so do play around with it, run a few commands, and get a feel for how it works.

Beyond Python - Other Essential Languages

Just as a linguist's ability to understand multiple languages provides them with greater depth and nuance in their understanding of culture and communication, knowing multiple programming languages can equip a prompt engineer with a versatile set of tools to tackle a wide array of problems. While Python is a key language for prompt engineering, there are others that serve important roles too.

JavaScript

If Python is the language of data science and machine learning, JavaScript is the lingua franca of the web. Many AI models are integrated into web applications, making JavaScript an essential language for prompt engineers working in this area. It allows engineers to make AI-powered websites, create interactive elements, or build front-end applications to showcase AI models.

Why JavaScript? It's because of its ability to support event-driven, functional, and imperative programming styles. This language is everywhere on the internet, running in your browser, in the cloud, and even on hardware.

For more information on JavaScript, check out Mozilla's JavaScript guide. https://developer.mozilla.org/en-US/docs/Web/JavaScript/Guide or its GitHub repository https://github.com/tc39/ecma262

SQL

When it comes to dealing with databases, SQL (Structured Query Language) is the standard. For prompt engineers working with large datasets, being able to query databases with SQL is a must-have skill. It allows you to access and manipulate data, extract insights, and feed relevant data into your AI models.

SQL is like the librarian of a vast library - it knows exactly where every piece of information is stored and can fetch it for you in no time. Its primary role is to handle structured data, i.e., data that is organized in tables.

More information about SQL can be found in its official documentation.
https://www.iso.org/standard/63555.html

R

Although Python holds the crown in the realm of machine learning, R is another language that is quite popular in the world of statistics and data analysis. It provides a wide variety of statistical and graphical techniques, including linear and nonlinear modelling, classical statistical tests, time-series analysis, classification, and clustering. This makes it a great tool for prompt engineers who are heavily involved in data analysis and pre-processing.

R has an extensive collection of packages, a vibrant community, and is open-source. For those interested in statistical and numerical analysis in AI, R is worth considering.

To learn more about R, you can refer to the official documentation.
https://www.r-project.org/other-docs.html)
and its GitHub repository
https://github.com/wch/r-source

HTML/CSS

While not programming languages in the traditional sense, HTML (Hypertext Markup Language) and CSS (Cascading Style Sheets) are essential for prompt engineers involved in developing user interfaces for AI applications. HTML is used for creating the structure of web pages, while CSS is used for styling and layout of web pages.

HTML/CSS skills are valuable for creating intuitive and user-friendly interfaces for AI systems, ensuring that users can interact with the underlying AI smoothly and effectively.

For a deep dive into HTML, you can refer to Mozilla's HTML guide.
https://developer.mozilla.org/en-US/docs/Web/HTML
and for CSS, you can refer to Mozilla's CSS guide
https://developer.mozilla.org/en-US/docs/Web/CSS

Docker

Docker is not a programming language but a platform that helps to develop, deploy, and run applications inside containers. It's essential for prompt engineers who need to deliver their AI models into production. Docker ensures that the application works uniformly, regardless of differences in the environments.

More information about Docker can be found in its official documentation. https://docs.docker.com/get-started/overview/ and its GitHub repository
https://github.com/docker

Shell scripting

Shell scripting can be a useful tool in the arsenal of any AI engineer, including a prompt engineer. Shell scripts, particularly in Unix-based systems like Linux, provide a way to automate tasks, manipulate files and directories, and manage system processes. They can be especially handy for setting up environments, automating data gathering and preprocessing tasks, and handling various other routine tasks.

To learn more about Shell scripting, you might find "The Beginner's Guide to Shell Scripting" useful.
https://www.linuxconfig.org/bash-scripting-tutorial-for-beginners

MATLAB

MATLAB (short for Matrix Laboratory) is a high-level language and environment designed specifically for numerical computation. It's particularly popular in academia and industries where extensive mathematical modelling is required, such as signal processing, communications, control systems, and computational finance. For prompt engineers working in these fields, MATLAB might be a useful tool to know.

The official MATLAB documentation can be found at: https://www.mathworks.com/help/matlab/

Keep in mind that these are just additional tools and languages that might be useful depending on your specific situation and the problems you're trying to solve. As with any tool, the key is to understand when and how to use them effectively.

By expanding your repertoire to include these languages, you can broaden your horizons and become a more adaptable and versatile prompt engineer. Remember, the art of prompt engineering isn't just about understanding AI models—it's also about integrating those models into the broader tech ecosystem.

Getting Hands-On

The best way to learn is by doing. So, roll up your sleeves—it's time to dive into some hands-on coding!

First, you will need to set up a Python environment and preferably choose an IDE.
If you are on a Linux machine it will have Python installed by default. Python in the wild can be version 2.x or 3.x. Modern Python and the one you should invest your time in is 3.x. Idle is the default Python editor that comes with the language and is simple yet powerful.

On Mac or Windows machines, you will need to install Python and an IDE.

For a good guide on this please either look at the Python website or here at Real Python.

https://www.python.org/
https://realpython.com/installing-python/

Hello, Python!

Let's start with the simplest program you can write in Python, the infamous "Hello, World!". In your Python environment, type the following command and see the magic happen.

```
print("Hello, World!")
```

Running this command will display the text "Hello, World!" on your screen. Congratulations! You've just written and executed your first Python program.

Data Play with Pandas

Pandas is a Python library that makes working with data a breeze. Let's try creating a simple DataFrame (the fundamental data structure in pandas), and perform some operations on it.

First, you'll need to import pandas:

```
import pandas as pd
```

Now let's create a DataFrame:

```
data = {
    'apples': [3, 2, 0, 1],
    'oranges': [0, 3, 7, 2]
}
purchases = pd.DataFrame(data)
print(purchases)
```

This will create a table of data showing the number of apples and oranges bought.

SQL Queries

SQL is a language used for interacting with databases. While it's a bit different from Python, it's no less important. Here's a simple SQL query that retrieves all records from a table named 'Users':

```sql
SELECT * FROM Users;
```

To run this query, you would need to be connected to a database with a table named 'Users'. It's simple, but from here, SQL gets much more powerful. You can filter, sort, and aggregate data in any way you can imagine.

These exercises are simple, but they are a start. They're designed to give you a taste of what it's like to work with these languages. As you delve deeper into your journey as a prompt engineer, you'll encounter more complex and exciting challenges. For now, familiarize yourself with these basics—they're your first steps into the world of prompt engineering!

For further learning, you might want to check out resources like Codecademy (https://www.codecademy.com/) and Coursera (https://www.coursera.org/). They offer interactive courses in Python, SQL, and more. Remember, learning to code is a journey. Enjoy the process and happy coding!

Python: Playing with Lists

Lists are a fundamental data structure in Python, used to store multiple items in a single variable. Let's create a list and manipulate it.

```python
# Create a list of fruits
fruits = ['apple', 'banana', 'cherry']
```

```
# Add a fruit to the list
fruits.append('orange')

# Remove a fruit from the list
fruits.remove('banana')

# Print the list
print(fruits)
```

This should output: ['apple', 'cherry', 'orange'].

NumPy: Creating and Manipulating Arrays

NumPy is a powerful library used for working with arrays. Let's create a simple NumPy array and perform an operation on it.

```
# Import NumPy
import numpy as np

# Create a NumPy array
array = np.array([1, 2, 3, 4, 5])

# Multiply every element in the array by 2
array = array * 2

# Print the array
print(array)
```

This should output: [2 4 6 8 10].

JavaScript: Saying Hello to the World

JavaScript is essential for adding dynamic behaviour to web pages.

You can write this code in a simple text editor although using an IDE can help with its syntax highlighting.

An excellent starter on javascript is at w3schools website.

https://www.w3schools.com/js/js_examples.asp

A good text editor and playground for starting in html and javascript is the jsfiddle website.
https://jsfiddle.net/

Let's try writing a simple JavaScript code snippet.

```
// Display an alert box with a message
alert("Hello, World!");
```

To run this code, you would need to add it to a JavaScript file linked to an HTML page, or directly within HTML script tags.

Don't worry if you don't understand everything at first—coding is about continuous learning and improvement. Keep experimenting and don't be afraid to make mistakes. As you continue to learn and explore, you'll become more comfortable with these languages and their respective syntax.

Remember, you can learn more about Python, NumPy, and other languages at their official documentation sites:

Python: Python Official Documentation at
https://www.python.org/

NumPy: NumPy Official Documentation at
 https://numpy.org/doc/

JavaScript: MDN Web Docs at
https://developer.mozilla.org/en-US/docs/Web/JavaScript

Also, online platforms like Kaggle and DataCamp offer interactive Python and SQL courses and exercises, which can be a great resource for hands-on learning. Keep exploring and practising, and you'll continue to grow as a prompt engineer!

Let's dive into some basic interactions with language models using Python and one of the most popular libraries for language processing tasks, Hugging Face's Transformers. The Transformers library provides easy access to pre-trained models for various natural language processing (NLP) tasks, including text generation, translation, summarization, and more.

Remember, to run the code provided, you need to install the necessary libraries. For this example, you'll need to install Transformers, which can be done in Linux using pip:

```
pip install transformers
```

Interacting with GPT-2 Using Transformers

We can use the GPT-2 model to generate text that continues a prompt we give it.

```python
from transformers import GPT2LMHeadModel, GPT2Tokenizer

# Initialize the tokenizer and the model
tokenizer = GPT2Tokenizer.from_pretrained("gpt2")
model = GPT2LMHeadModel.from_pretrained("gpt2")

# Define a text prompt
prompt = "Once upon a time, in a land far away,"

# Encode the text prompt and generate the text
input_ids = tokenizer.encode(prompt, return_tensors="pt")
output = model.generate(input_ids, max_length=100,
temperature=0.7, num_return_sequences=1)

# Decode the output
generated_text = tokenizer.decode(output[:,
input_ids.shape[-1]:][0], skip_special_tokens=True)

# Print the generated text
print(generated_text)
```

The "gpt2" in the 'from_pretrained' function refers to the version of the GPT-2 model that we're using. You can change this to use different versions of GPT-2, or even entirely different models.

The 'generate' function is where the magic happens—it takes in your prompt and generates a continuation of it. The parameters such as 'max_length', 'temperature', and 'num_return_sequences' allow you to control aspects of the text generation, such as the length of the generated text, the randomness (higher temperature = more randomness), and the number of different text sequences to generate, respectively.

To learn more about the Hugging Face Transformers library and other available models, you can refer to the Hugging Face Transformers Official Documentation. https://huggingface.co/docs/transformers/index

To practice writing and running code interactively, consider using a platform like Google Colab found online at https://colab.research.google.com/ This provides a cloud-based Python programming environment and supports the execution of machine learning code.

Remember, the best way to learn is to experiment and explore! Don't be afraid to change the prompt, adjust the parameters, or try out different models.
Remember, the best way to learn is to experiment and explore! Don't be afraid to change the prompt, adjust the parameters, or try out different models.

Fine-tuning a Language Model for a Specific Task

One of the most powerful aspects of language models like GPT-2 or GPT-3 is that they can be fine-tuned for specific tasks. For example, let's consider the task of sentiment analysis, where we want to determine if a given piece of text has a positive, negative, or neutral sentiment.

While GPT-2 isn't designed for sentiment analysis out of the box, we can fine-tune it on a dataset of labelled sentiment data so that it can perform this task. The details of fine-tuning involve some more advanced concepts and require a good amount of computational resources, so we won't cover the actual code here. However, a general outline of the process is as follows:

1. Collect a labelled dataset for your task (in this case, a set of text examples each labelled as positive, negative, or neutral).
2. Divide your dataset into a training set and a validation set.
3. Load a pre-trained version of GPT-2 using Hugging Face's Transformers library.
4. Train (also known as 'fine-tuning') the GPT-2 model on your training dataset, adjusting the weights of the model to minimize the difference between the model's predictions and the actual labels.
5. Regularly evaluate the model's performance on the validation set to ensure it's not just memorizing the training data (a problem known as overfitting).
6. Once the model's performance on the validation set stops improving, stop training. You now have a fine-tuned model!

For more details and tutorials on how to fine-tune language models with the Transformers library, refer to the Hugging Face Transformers Official Documentation.

Building a Chatbot

Language models can be also used to build chatbots. Using a model like DialoGPT (a variant of GPT-2 specifically fine-tuned for dialogue), you can create a chatbot that generates human-like responses to given inputs. Here's a very simple example of how you might do this:

```
from transformers import AutoModelForCausalLM,
AutoTokenizer

tokenizer = AutoTokenizer.from_pretrained("microsoft/
DialoGPT-medium")
model = AutoModelForCausalLM.from_pretrained("microsoft/
DialoGPT-medium")

# Let's chat for 5 lines
for step in range(5):
    # encode the new user input, add the eos_token and return a
tensor in Pytorch
    new_user_input_ids = tokenizer.encode(input(">> User:") +
tokenizer.eos_token, return_tensors='pt')

    # append the new user input tokens to the chat history
    bot_input_ids = torch.cat([chat_history_ids,
new_user_input_ids], dim=-1) if step > 0 else
new_user_input_ids

    # generated a response while limiting the total chat history
to 1000 tokens,
    chat_history_ids = model.generate(bot_input_ids,
max_length=1000, pad_token_id=tokenizer.eos_token_id)

    # pretty print last output tokens from bot
    print("DialoGPT:
{}".format(tokenizer.decode(chat_history_ids[:,
bot_input_ids.shape[-1]:][0], skip_special_tokens=True)))
```

In the code above, the user input is tokenized and combined with the chat history to form the bot's input. The bot then generates a response, which is appended to the chat history. This process repeats for a number of turns.

Creating a Text Generator

An interesting application of language models is generating creative text, such as stories or poems. Let's create a very basic text generator using GPT-2:

```python
from transformers import GPT2LMHeadModel, GPT2Tokenizer

tokenizer = GPT2Tokenizer.from_pretrained("gpt2")
model = GPT2LMHeadModel.from_pretrained("gpt2")

# Define a prompt
prompt = "Once upon a time, "

# Encode the prompt and generate text
inputs = tokenizer.encode(prompt, return_tensors="pt")
outputs = model.generate(inputs, max_length=150,
do_sample=True, temperature=0.7)

# Decode and print the generated text
generated_text = tokenizer.decode(outputs[0],
skip_special_tokens=True)
print(generated_text)
```

This script takes a prompt ("Once upon a time, ") and generates a piece of text based on that prompt. The 'max_length' parameter controls the length of the generated text, and the 'temperature' parameter controls the randomness of the generation process.

Predicting the Next Word

A core capability of language models is predicting the next word in a sentence. Here's a simple example of how you can do this with GPT-2:

```
from transformers import GPT2LMHeadModel, GPT2Tokenizer

tokenizer = GPT2Tokenizer.from_pretrained("gpt2")
model = GPT2LMHeadModel.from_pretrained("gpt2")

sentence = "The quick brown fox jumps over the "

# Encode the sentence and get the model's prediction
inputs = tokenizer.encode(sentence, return_tensors="pt")
predictions = model(inputs).logits

# Get the predicted token ID and decode it into a word
predicted_token_id = torch.argmax(predictions[:, -1, :]).item()
predicted_word = tokenizer.decode([predicted_token_id])

print(predicted_word)
```

This script takes a sentence and predicts what the next word in the sentence will be. This is an example of the kind of language understanding that underlies the power of language models like GPT-2 and GPT-3.

Remember, these are simplified examples. When working with real-world applications, you will need to consider various additional factors such as handling different types of inputs, managing longer conversations, and handling different languages or domains of knowledge.

To dive deeper into using the Transformers library and fine-tuning language models, I recommend checking out the tutorials in the Hugging Face Transformers Official Documentation and the Hugging Face Model Hub, which has pre-trained models for a wide variety of tasks.

Remember, the key to learning to code is practice. Don't worry if you don't get these exercises right on your first try. Debugging and resolving issues is a significant part of the learning process. Keep trying, and you'll get the hang of it!

Resources for Further Learning

As the final part of this chapter, let's guide you to some excellent resources where you can continue your journey of learning Python, AI, and other languages pertinent to prompt engineering. These resources range from online courses and tutorials to books and interactive platforms, offering you a variety of options based on your preferred learning style.

Online Courses

Codecademy: Codecademy provides interactive learning experiences in various programming languages, including Python and JavaScript.
https://www.codecademy.com/

Coursera: Coursera offers a multitude of online courses from universities and companies around the world. There are numerous courses available on Python, machine learning, AI, and more.
https://www.coursera.org/

Kaggle: While known for its data science competitions, Kaggle also offers "micro-courses" on Python, machine learning, SQL, and more.
https://www.kaggle.com/

edX: edX, like Coursera, which offers online courses from many top universities and institutes. It offers a professional certificate in Python for Data Science.
https://www.edx.org/

Books

Python Crash Course: This book is a fast-paced, thorough

introduction to Python that will have you writing programs, solving problems, and making things that work in no time. https://nostarch.com/pythoncrashcourse2e

Hands-On Machine Learning with Scikit-Learn, Keras, and TensorFlow: This book by Aurélien Géron provides a practical approach to learning machine learning using Python and popular libraries. More information is available at https://www.oreilly.com/library/view/hands-on-machine-learning/9781492032632/

Communities

Stack Overflow: A community of developers answering all sorts of coding questions, including those about Python and AI. https://stackoverflow.com/

Reddit: The LearnPython subreddit is a friendly community for Python learners to share their knowledge and learn from others. https://www.reddit.com/r/learnpython/

GitHub: Open source community to explore real-world projects, contribute, and collaborate with other developers. https://github.com/

Remember, the key to mastering Python, AI, and prompt engineering is continuous learning and practice. The more you interact with these resources, the more you will understand and the better you will get.

Natural Language Processing: The Art Of Teaching Machines To Talk

Have you ever tried to learn a new language? Remember how it wasn't just about learning words and grammar, but also understanding the context, idioms, and even the culture behind it? Now, imagine trying to teach that to a machine. Welcome to the fascinating world of Natural Language Processing (NLP)!

NLP is like a charismatic translator who can flawlessly navigate between the languages of humans and machines. This field, lying at the intersection of linguistics, computer science, and AI, is all about enabling machines to understand, process, and generate human language. In other words, it's about teaching machines to talk!

At the heart of NLP, there are tasks like speech recognition (transcribing human speech into written text), natural language understanding (interpreting the meaning of the text), and natural language generation (creating meaningful sentences). These tasks might sound simple for us humans, but for machines, it's a whole different ball game.

Take, for example, the phrase "It's raining cats and dogs." To a machine, this might initially seem like a bizarre meteorological event involving pets. But through NLP, we teach the AI that this phrase is an idiom that means it's raining heavily. It's like playing charades with a machine, and the more it plays, the better it gets at understanding our clues.

In the realm of NLP, every day is a new opportunity to bridge the gap between human language and machine comprehension. As we delve deeper into NLP, you'll gain insights into its complexities and its marvels, equipping you to design more intelligent and intuitive prompts.

By the end of this section, you'll understand how machines dissect our language, how they learn the nuanced dance of human conversation, and how you, as a prompt engineer, can lead them through this dance. So, let's get this conversation started!

Introduction to Natural Language Processing (NLP)

In this subsection, we introduce the concept of Natural Language Processing (NLP), emphasizing its role as the link between human language and machine understanding. We will touch upon what NLP is, its importance in today's AI-driven world, and how it enables machines to understand, process, and even generate human language.

Speech Recognition: Turning Sound into Sense

In the heart of bustling city streets or a quiet suburban home, you can often hear, "Hey Siri" or "Alexa, play my favourite songs." This magic, where machines seemingly understand our spoken words and respond to us, is powered by Speech Recognition. It's like having your personal transcriber, ready to jot down your every word, but one that lives inside your devices!

Speech recognition is the first step in the dance of Natural Language Processing. It's where machines make sense of sound waves and turn them into written words. Imagine being at a crowded party, with loud music and everyone talking at once. Amid this cacophony, your friend tells you an interesting story. Somehow, your brain manages to filter out the noise and understand your friend's words. That's quite a remarkable feat, isn't it? Now, imagine teaching a machine to do the same. Sounds tough, right? But, that's exactly what speech recognition technology accomplishes.

Let's simplify the process. When we speak, we produce sound waves. These sound waves, when captured by a microphone, are transformed into digital data that the machine can understand. The speech recognition systems then try to match these digital sound patterns with the patterns of words or phrases it already knows. It's akin to a child learning to match a picture of an apple with the word 'apple'.

To further illustrate, let's look at our trusty voice assistants like Siri, Alexa, or Google Assistant. When you say, "What's the weather like today?" these voice assistants capture your voice, convert the speech into text, and then process the text to give you the desired information. And voila, you get your answer without having to type a single letter!

The world of speech recognition is indeed magical and complex. But remember, it's just the first step in our fascinating journey of Natural Language Processing. With each stride, we'll venture deeper into the realm of machines and language.

For those who wish to delve further into the technical aspects of speech recognition, the Speech Recognition page on Wikipedia (https://en.wikipedia.org/wiki/Speech_recognition) is a good starting point. For a more detailed understanding, you can also explore the official documentation for Google's Speech-to-Text API. https://cloud.google.com/speech-to-text/docs

Natural Language Understanding

After transcribing human speech into written text, the next step in NLP is to understand the meaning of that text. This phase is known as Natural Language Understanding (NLU).

Remember the phrase "It's raining cats and dogs"? Even though speech recognition can transcribe this sentence perfectly, it's still a mystery to the machine. It needs to understand that this phrase is not about pets falling from the sky, but an idiom meaning it's raining heavily. This is where NLU comes into play.

NLU is like a detective, deciphering the meaning behind the words. It tries to understand the context, the sentiment, the intent behind the message, and much more. It understands that "I am feeling blue" does not mean someone is turning blue, but rather, they are feeling sad.

Let's take our voice assistant example again. When you ask, "What's the weather like today?" after transcribing your voice into text, NLU comes into play. The assistant needs to understand that you are seeking information about the weather for the current day. This understanding enables it to respond appropriately.

NLU also plays a crucial role in chatbots, customer service automation, and any application where the machine needs to understand the user's intent. It's the part of NLP that makes our interactions with machines feel more 'human'.

Understanding the mechanics of NLU is like deciphering the Rosetta Stone of human language for machines. It's an intricate process, full of complexities and subtleties, but one that is essential for the magic of NLP.

For further reading on Natural Language Understanding, you can check out the Wikipedia page https://en.wikipedia.org/wiki/Natural-language_understanding

Also, the documentation for Google's Natural Language API offers a closer look at how machines understand human language. https://cloud.google.com/natural-language/docs

Natural Language Generation

So, machines have learned to listen and understand, but can they speak? The answer is yes, and it's all thanks to Natural Language Generation (NLG). NLG is like the voice of the machines—it's the technology that enables them to generate meaningful and contextually appropriate responses.

You can think of NLG as the final piece of the NLP puzzle, where machines go from passive listeners to active participants in a conversation. After understanding the user's intent (thanks to NLU), NLG crafts a relevant response. It's like the machine is writing its own script on the fly!

Remember our voice assistant example? When you ask, "What's the weather like today?", the assistant, after understanding your query, uses NLG to construct a response like, "The weather today is sunny with a high of 25 degrees."

In the realm of chatbots, NLG is what enables the bot to respond to user queries dynamically. Whether it's providing information, solving problems, or even engaging in small talk, NLG breathes life into these conversations.

However, it's important to note that NLG is not about crafting perfect sentences—it's about crafting the right sentences. The goal is to generate responses that meet the user's needs and feel natural in the conversation. And that's what makes it such an exciting and important area of NLP.

Understanding NLG is like understanding how machines find their voice. It's a captivating process that brings us one step closer to seamless human-machine interactions.

For a deeper dive into Natural Language Generation, check out its Wikipedia page. https://en.wikipedia.org/wiki/Natural_language_generation

Additionally, you can visit OpenAI's GPT-3 page to understand how advanced language models generate human-like text. https://openai.com/research/gpt-3

Sentiment Analysis: Reading Between the Lines

In a conversation, words are just the tip of the iceberg. The meaning often lies not just in what is said, but how it is said—the emotional undertone that accompanies the words. This is where Sentiment Analysis, also known as opinion mining or emotion AI, comes in.

Sentiment Analysis is like the empath in the world of NLP. It goes beyond the words and tries to understand the emotions and attitudes behind them. For instance, consider the phrases "I love this movie" and "I hate this movie." The words "love" and "hate" here indicate the sentiment of the speaker towards the movie.

In the context of business, Sentiment Analysis plays a key role in understanding customer attitudes. Companies use it to analyze customer feedback, social media conversations, and product reviews to gain insights into customer satisfaction and brand perception.

For prompt engineers, understanding Sentiment Analysis can provide valuable insights into how users might feel when interacting with an AI system. This can help design more empathetic and responsive prompts.

But it's not always as simple as looking for "happy" or "sad" words. Language is complex, and sentiments can be nuanced. A phrase can be sarcastic, ambiguous, or context-dependent, which can make Sentiment Analysis quite a challenging task. But as they say, no pain, no gain!

To explore more about Sentiment Analysis, you can check out the Wikipedia page on the topic. https://en.wikipedia.org/wiki/Sentiment_analysis

For an in-depth understanding, you might want to visit Stanford University's Sentiment Analysis resource. http://nlp.stanford.edu/sentiment/index.html

Machine Translation: Breaking Down Language Barriers

If you've ever used a tool like Google Translate to understand a webpage in a foreign language, you've used machine translation. It's like having a multilingual friend who is always ready to help you understand different languages.

Machine translation is a fascinating area of NLP that aims to convert text or speech from one language to another automatically. The goal is to capture the meaning of the original text and reproduce it in the target language, all while maintaining the nuances and context of the original content. Simple, right? Well, not exactly!

Language is complex and full of idiosyncrasies. Direct word-for-word translations often miss the mark because the meaning of a phrase can depend heavily on its cultural and contextual nuances. Think about idioms or slang, for example. A phrase like "break a leg" in English might perplex a machine if taken literally!

Modern machine translation, like Google's Neural Machine Translation system, uses sophisticated AI models to capture these nuances. These systems are trained on vast amounts of text in multiple languages, learning the intricacies of human language, one translation at a time.

As a prompt engineer, understanding machine translation can help you design prompts that can cross linguistic boundaries. You can create AI systems that are inclusive and accessible to users from different linguistic backgrounds.

For further exploration of Machine Translation, you might want to visit its Wikipedia page.
https://en.wikipedia.org/wiki/Machine_translation

For more advanced study, the Association for Machine Translation in the Americas (AMTA) offers resources and events.
 https://amtaweb.org/

The Mechanics of NLP

Here, we will delve into the core tasks that constitute NLP, such as speech recognition, natural language understanding, and natural language generation. We will offer a high-level overview of how machines perform these tasks, transforming spoken or written language into a form that they can understand and respond to. We'll demystify these processes without diving too deep into the technicalities.

Understanding Language - The Basics of NLP

At the heart of human interaction lies language - a complex web of meanings, codes, and symbols that we navigate with ease. For machines, however, this web isn't so simple. That's where Natural Language Processing (NLP) steps in, like a skilled guide, helping machines to comprehend and traverse this intricate landscape.

NLP is a branch of artificial intelligence that focuses on the interaction between humans and machines through natural language. It's about enabling our digital counterparts to understand, interpret, process, and respond to human language in a valuable way. From voice assistants to automatic translations, NLP plays a pivotal role in numerous technologies we use daily.

But what makes NLP so challenging? Consider the number of languages we have, and the variety of tones, contexts, idioms, and cultural nuances embedded in each. Now, imagine teaching a machine to understand all these subtleties. That's what makes NLP a fascinating field. It's about teaching machines not just to understand our words but the meaning behind those words.

Let's illustrate this with an example. Take the word 'bat.' It's a simple three-letter word but has multiple meanings. It could be a nocturnal creature, sports equipment, or even a verb denoting action. The way we humans effortlessly identify the right meaning based on context is a cognitive marvel. Teaching a machine to emulate this cognitive function is one of the significant challenges in NLP.

Now, why is NLP so critical in AI? Because communication forms the basis of intelligent behaviour. With NLP, machines can analyze feedback, understand commands, provide recommendations, and even participate in conversations! By mastering language, AI becomes more accessible and useful, gradually transforming our world.

For a deeper dive into the fascinating world of NLP, you may find the following resources helpful:

Stanford University's Natural Language Processing Course
https://online.stanford.edu/courses/cs224n-natural-language-processing-deep-learning

Natural Language Processing with Python book by Steven Bird, Ewan Klein, and Edward Loper
http://www.nltk.org/book/

Google's Machine Learning Crash Course:
https://developers.google.com/machine-learning/crash-course/natural-language-processing/video-lecture

Wikipedia page on Natural Language Processing
https://en.wikipedia.org/wiki/Natural_language_processing

In the following sections, we'll delve into the specifics of various NLP tasks, shedding light on how machines understand and generate human language.

An Introduction to Speech Recognition

Have you ever wondered how your voice assistant, be it Siri, Alexa, or Google Assistant, recognizes your voice commands and responds? How can they transcribe your spoken words into text, understand it, and then generate an appropriate response? Welcome to the world of Speech Recognition!

At its core, Speech Recognition is all about converting spoken language into written text. It's the first step in how machines understand our vocal commands. Think of it as teaching a machine to listen and jot down notes, except, these notes are a bit more complex than the ones you took in school.

So, how does Speech Recognition work? Without getting too technical, let's outline the general process:

Acoustic Processing
In this step, the speech signal is captured and processed to extract acoustic features like pitch and volume. It's like a machine trying

to understand the distinct sounds in your speech.

Phonetic Classification

The processed acoustic signal is then mapped to phonetic units or phonemes (the smallest unit of sound). Here, the machine is trying to understand the building blocks of your words.

Word Recognition

Finally, these phonemes are put together to form words and phrases based on a language model. It's where the machine begins to see the bigger picture of what you're saying.

Let's consider a simple example - you say, "Hey Siri, play my favourite song." Siri captures your speech, processes it, and converts it into written text. Then, using NLP, it understands your command and plays your favourite song. It's an intricate dance of technologies, with Speech Recognition leading.

Of course, this is a simplified explanation. In reality, Speech Recognition involves more sophisticated technologies like Hidden Markov Models and Neural Networks. But, at its heart, it's all about transforming human speech into a format machines can understand.

If you're interested in exploring Speech Recognition in more detail, you might find these resources useful:

DeepSpeech GitHub page by Mozilla. It's an open-source Speech Recognition Tool
https://github.com/mozilla/DeepSpeech

Speech and Language Processing, a book by Daniel Jurafsky and James H. Martin
https://web.stanford.edu/~jurafsky/slp3/

RealPython's tutorial on "An Intro to Speech Recognition in Python"
https://realpython.com/python-speech-recognition/

Wikipedia's page on Speech Recognition:

https://en.wikipedia.org/wiki/Speech_recognition

As we continue, we'll explore how machines not only understand our spoken words but also interpret the meaning behind them. It's time for machines to read between the lines!

The Art of Interpretation - Natural Language Understanding

Imagine you're talking to a friend about a movie you recently watched. You say, "The plot was a rollercoaster ride!" Your friend, understanding the idiom, knows you're referring to the plot being full of unexpected twists and turns. But how would a machine interpret this phrase? This is where Natural Language Understanding (NLU) comes into play.

NLU is a sub-discipline of NLP that focuses on machine reading comprehension. It goes beyond merely transcribing speech or parsing text—it's about understanding the intent, context, and overall meaning of the words. Essentially, NLU is the process that helps machines read between the lines.

The complexity of NLU can't be overstated. Human language is rife with idioms, cultural nuances, implied meanings, and other complexities. Teaching a machine to understand all this is like teaching someone a new language, with all its linguistic quirks and peculiarities.

So, how do machines do this? Again, without diving deep into the technical details, the process of NLU generally involves

Parsing
This involves breaking down a sentence into its grammatical components—like nouns, verbs, adjectives, etc. It's like a machine figuring out the basic structure of your sentence.

Semantic Analysis
In this step, the machine determines the meanings of the words and how they combine to create meaning in a sentence. For our movie example, it's about recognizing that "rollercoaster ride"

45

refers to an experience full of ups and downs, not an actual amusement park ride.

Contextual Interpretation

Finally, the machine interprets the overall context of the conversation. This could involve understanding the subject matter, recognizing references to earlier parts of the conversation, and even picking up on cultural or social norms.

Using our movie example, a machine equipped with NLU capabilities would understand that "rollercoaster ride" in this context refers to an unpredictable, thrilling plot, not a literal rollercoaster ride.

Interested in diving deeper into the world of NLU? Check out the following resources:

Natural Language Understanding by James Allen - a comprehensive book on the subject
https://www.amazon.com/Natural-Language-Understanding-James-Allen/dp/0805303340

An introduction to Natural Language Understanding by Analytics Vidhya
https://www.analyticsvidhya.com/blog/2019/07/how-get-started-nlp-6-unique-ways-perform-tokenization/

Stanford University's course on Natural Language Processing with Deep Learning
https://www.youtube.com/playlist?list=PL3FW7Lu3i5Jsnh1rnUwq_TcylNr7EkRe6

Wikipedia's page on Natural Language Understanding
https://en.wikipedia.org/wiki/Natural-language_understanding

As we continue, we'll explore how machines not only understand our language but also generate human-like responses. It's time to turn our machines into chatterboxes!

Crafting Responses - Natural Language Generation

So far, we've seen how machines can recognize and understand our language. But, how do they craft responses that mimic human conversation? This is where Natural Language Generation (NLG) takes centre stage.

NLG is the task of converting information from computer databases or semantic intents into readable, human-like language. It's the process that allows our digital assistants to generate responses to our questions or requests. If Speech Recognition and Natural Language Understanding are about input, NLG is all about output.

Consider this: you ask your voice assistant, "What's the weather like today?" It understands your question, retrieves the relevant information, and then responds, "The weather today is sunny with a high of 25 degrees." This response is generated by NLG.

At its core, NLG involves the following steps:

Data Aggregation

The machine gathers the necessary data to construct its response. This might involve retrieving data from a weather forecast database, for example.

Text Planning: The machine decides how to structure its response. In the weather forecast example, it might decide to mention the weather condition first ("sunny") and then the temperature ("a high of 25 degrees").

Sentence Construction

The machine constructs the sentences of its response, ensuring they are grammatically correct and fluent.

The goal of NLG is to produce text that is indistinguishable from that written by a human. With advancements in AI and machine learning, machines are getting better and better at this, generating everything from weather forecasts to news articles, to stories.

Here are some resources to dive deeper into NLG:

A Gentle Introduction to Natural Language Generation: https://machinelearningmastery.com/a-gentle-introduction-to-natural-language-generation/

Natural Language Generation: https://en.wikipedia.org/wiki/Natural_language_generation

NLG in Customer Communication: https://towardsdatascience.com/nlg-in-customer-communication-35a89f6df4c2

In the next section, we'll delve into some other key NLP tasks, like Sentiment Analysis and Machine Translation. But by now, it's clear that NLP is truly a marvel, equipping machines with the power to understand and speak our language!

Reading Between the Lines - Sentiment Analysis

Imagine you're reading a review for a restaurant. The reviewer says, "The ambience was great, but the food was an absolute disaster." Even though the statement about the ambience is positive, you'd probably understand that the reviewer had a negative experience because of the latter part of the sentence. This is a simple sentiment analysis task, something we humans do without even thinking about it. But how does a machine approach this task?

Welcome to Sentiment Analysis, also known as opinion mining or emotion AI. Sentiment analysis is a Natural Language Processing task that determines the emotional tone behind words. It's used to identify and extract subjective information from source materials.

At a basic level, sentiment analysis could simply classify text as 'positive', 'negative', or 'neutral'. However, it can also be more nuanced, identifying emotions such as 'happy', 'frustrated', 'angry', etc.

Let's consider a practical application of sentiment analysis. Businesses often use it to understand customer opinions and feedback. If a company launches a new product, it could use sentiment analysis to sift through social media posts or product reviews to understand how well the product is being received.

Sentiment analysis is a fascinating, albeit challenging, aspect of NLP. It requires the machine not just to understand the words, but to 'read between the lines'.

Here are some resources to delve deeper into sentiment analysis:

A Beginner's Guide to Sentiment Analysis:
https://monkeylearn.com/sentiment-analysis/

Sentiment Analysis: Nearly Everything You Need to Know:
https://www.kdnuggets.com/2018/08/sentiment-analysis-nlp-text-analytics-deep-learning.html

Sentiment Analysis with Python:
https://realpython.com/sentiment-analysis-python/

In the next sub-section, we'll explore another fascinating NLP task: Machine Translation.

Crossing Language Barriers - Machine Translation

In today's globally connected world, communication often needs to cross language barriers. This is where machine translation comes in. Machine translation is an application of NLP that focuses on converting text or speech from one language to another.

Remember using an online translator to help with your foreign language homework? That's machine translation in action! These translators are more than just a dictionary converting words from one language to another. They are designed to understand the structure, grammar, and nuances of languages, enabling them to provide a more accurate translation.

Machine translation works through different techniques, ranging from rule-based methods, where linguistic rules and bilingual dictionaries are used, to statistical methods, which rely on the analysis of large bilingual text corpora. More recently, neural networks and deep learning have been employed to further improve translation quality.

Google Translate is one of the most well-known applications of machine translation, supporting translation between 100+ languages. It uses a technology called Neural Machine Translation (NMT), where deep neural networks 'learn' translations based on a vast amount of data.

Despite the advancements, machine translation isn't perfect and often struggles with idioms, cultural nuances, and context. However, it's a rapidly evolving field with researchers around the world working to refine these systems further.

Here are some resources for you to explore more about Machine Translation:

A Gentle Introduction to Neural Machine Translation: https://machinelearningmastery.com/introduction-neural-machine-translation/

Google's Neural Machine Translation System: https://ai.googleblog.com/2016/09/a-neural-network-for-machine.html

Machine Translation - Stanford University: https://nlp.stanford.edu/projects/nmt/

We hope this sub-section provided you with a high-level understanding of machine translation. In the next section, we will explore the real-world applications of Natural Language

Processing.

Challenges in NLP

Language is a beautifully complex system of communication. It's full of idioms, slang, dialects, cultural references, and context that vary wildly from place to place, person to person, and situation to situation. For us humans, these intricacies are part of what makes language rich and engaging. For machines, however, these nuances pose significant challenges.

Understanding Context

The meaning of a word can change drastically depending on the context in which it's used. For instance, the word 'bat' can refer to a piece of sports equipment or a nocturnal flying mammal, depending on the context. Teaching machines to understand such contextual differences is a major challenge in NLP.

Handling Ambiguity

Homonyms (words that are spelt and pronounced the same but have different meanings) and polysemy (words that have multiple related meanings) can be particularly tricky for NLP systems to navigate. Consider the sentence, "The bank raised its rates." Without more context, a machine might struggle to determine whether 'bank' refers to a financial institution or the side of a river.

Detecting Sarcasm and Irony

Sarcasm and irony are sophisticated language uses where the intended meaning is often the opposite of the literal meaning. These can be very difficult for NLP systems to detect, as they require an understanding of subtleties and cues that machines often miss.

Grasping Idioms and Cultural References

Phrases like 'kick the bucket' or 'let the cat out of the bag' can be baffling for machines as their literal meanings have little to do with their actual implications. Similarly, cultural references that are common knowledge among humans might not be understood by an AI system.

Managing Errors

Real-world data is often messy and full of errors. Misspellings, abbreviations, and grammatical mistakes are common in written text, while speech data can contain stuttering, background noise, and variations in accent and pronunciation. NLP systems need to be robust enough to handle these errors.

Despite these challenges, researchers are constantly developing more sophisticated NLP models and techniques. They're using advanced concepts like deep learning, context-based models, and reinforcement learning to help machines understand human language better. While we've made significant progress, there's still a long way to go before machines can fully grasp the richness and complexity of human language.

For more detailed insights into the challenges in NLP, you can check out the following resources:

Challenges in Natural Language Processing:
https://www.frontiersin.org/research-topics/4818/challenges-in-natural-language-processing

Why Natural Language Processing is complicated:
https://towardsdatascience.com/why-is-natural-language-processing-difficult-c4774e5b7a2f

Ten challenges in highly-interactive dialogue systems:
https://aclanthology.org/N19-2016/

In the next sub-section, we will discuss the applications of NLP in various industries, illustrating the wide range of uses for this technology.

NLP in Action

Natural Language Processing is the driving force behind many of the technological advancements we use daily. By enabling machines to understand human language, NLP has not only made our interactions with technology more natural and intuitive, but it has also opened up a myriad of applications across various industries. Here are some examples:

Voice Assistants: Amazon's Alexa, Apple's Siri, and Google Assistant - these voice-activated personal assistants are powered by NLP. They use speech recognition to understand our commands, natural language understanding to process what we're asking, and natural language generation to respond in a human-like manner. To learn more about how voice assistants work, you can visit the following resources:

Amazon Alexa: How It Works - Official Documentation (https://developer.amazon.com/en-US/alexa/alexa-voice-service/how-avs-works)

Behind the Scenes of Siri - Apple Developer Documentation (https://developer.apple.com/documentation/sirikit)

Machine Translation

Companies like Google and Microsoft use NLP to power their translation services, making it easier for people to communicate across language barriers. Google Translate, for example, uses advanced NLP techniques to convert text from one language to another. To explore this further:

Inside Google Translate - Google AI Blog (https://ai.googleblog.com/2020/06/recent-advances-in-google-translate.html)

Sentiment Analysis

Companies use sentiment analysis to gauge public opinion about their products and services. Twitter, for instance, uses NLP to categorize tweets as positive, negative, or neutral, giving companies valuable insight into customer sentiment. For more on this:

Sentiment Analysis: What it is and Why it's Used - MonkeyLearn Blog (https://monkeylearn.com/sentiment-analysis/)

Information Extraction

Search engines like Google use NLP to understand and index the billions of pages on the internet. NLP techniques help extract useful information and match it to user queries, making search more effective and relevant. Read more about this:

How Google Search Works - Google Search Documentation (https://www.google.com/search/howsearchworks/)

Content Recommendation

Platforms like Netflix and YouTube use NLP to analyze the content you consume and recommend similar items. They analyze user data, subtitles, descriptions, and other text-based information to understand user preferences and make more accurate recommendations. For a deeper understanding:

How Netflix Recommends Shows and Movies - Netflix Help Center (https://help.netflix.com/en/node/100639)

These are just a few examples of how NLP is changing the way we interact with technology and information. As we continue to improve our NLP techniques, we can expect to see even more exciting applications in the future.

NLP and Prompt Engineering

Natural Language Processing (NLP) plays a pivotal role in prompt engineering. By enabling machines to understand and generate human language, NLP allows us to communicate with AI models and receive meaningful responses. It is the foundation on which we build our prompts and interpret the AI's output. Let's break this down.

Crafting Effective Prompts

Understanding the principles of NLP helps us create prompts that the AI model can comprehend and respond to effectively. For instance, clear and specific prompts generally yield better results than vague or ambiguous ones. Additionally, understanding how a model interprets language can help us anticipate potential misinterpretations and adjust our prompts accordingly. To delve deeper into crafting effective prompts, you may explore the following resource:

"How to Write Prompts for AI Models" - OpenAI Blog [https://openai.com/blog/better-language-models/#howdoiuse]

Interpreting AI Responses

AI models like GPT-4 generate responses based on their understanding of language and the specific prompt they've received. Knowledge of NLP allows us to better interpret these responses, understand their limitations, and adjust our interaction strategy accordingly. You may find the following resource useful for further understanding:

"Decoding the Language of AI" - Medium Blog Post [https://medium.com/decode-ai/]

Advanced NLP in AI Models

Advanced NLP techniques like sentiment analysis, text classification, and named entity recognition play a crucial role in developing more nuanced AI models. These models are not only capable of understanding and generating text, but they also possess a level of contextual awareness, enabling them to interact in a more human-like manner. Here are some resources for further exploration:

"Sentiment Analysis and its Applications" - MonkeyLearn Blog [https://monkeylearn.com/sentiment-analysis/]

"Understanding Named Entity Recognition" - Towards Data Science Blog [https://towardsdatascience.com/named-entity-recognition-3fad3f53c91e]

Understanding NLP is crucial for anyone looking to work with AI language models, and it can be particularly helpful for prompt engineers. It's not about becoming an NLP expert, but rather about gaining enough knowledge to communicate effectively with AI and derive maximum benefit from its capabilities. As we continue to develop and refine NLP techniques, we can look forward to AI models that understand and generate language with even greater sophistication

Data Analysis And Interpretation: The Crystal Ball Of Ai

Setting out on the path of data analysis and interpretation is akin to morphing into a contemporary Sherlock Holmes. But rather than resolving mysterious crimes, you're delving into the depths of data, deciphering valuable insights that inform your prompt engineering decisions.

In the realm of AI and prompt engineering, the ability to analyze and interpret data is indispensable. It's through this process of data investigation that we can evaluate the performance of our AI models, pinpoint areas for potential improvement, and refine our prompts for superior outcomes.

Data analysis is akin to your crystal ball. Yet, instead of providing obscure images or hazy predictions, it presents clear, actionable insights. The process encompasses several stages: data collection, cleaning, transformation, and modelling, all aimed at uncovering pertinent information, deriving conclusions, and guiding decision-making.

Data analysis enables us to answer vital questions such as: How is our AI model performing? Which types of prompts yield the most engaging responses? What are the areas ripe for optimization and improvement? The objective isn't to metamorphose into a data scientist; it's about learning to harness data as a potent instrument in your prompt engineering toolkit.

To aid in understanding the importance and the process of data analysis, the book "Data Science for Dummies" by Lillian Pierson provides a straightforward, comprehensive overview.

Data Science for Dummies
https://www.amazon.com/Data-Science-Dummies-Lillian-Pierson/dp/1118841557

In the following subsections, we will further dissect the process of data analysis, examine each stage in more detail and explore their role in prompt engineering. We'll also delve into real-world applications of data analysis, offering tangible examples of how this process can enhance the efficacy of AI models and prompts.

The Importance of Data Analysis in AI

Data analysis plays a pivotal role in the field of artificial intelligence. It provides the foundation for understanding how our AI models perform and gives us the tools to continually refine and optimize these models.

A core part of AI's functionality is its ability to learn from data and make predictions or decisions based on that data. For example, a chatbot might learn to generate more relevant responses by analyzing data from previous interactions. Without data analysis, this learning process wouldn't be possible.

Data analysis allows us to evaluate the performance of our AI models quantitatively. By analyzing the data, we can measure how accurately the model predicts outcomes and identify areas for improvement. For example, if an AI model is designed to predict stock prices, data analysis could reveal how closely the model's predictions align with actual prices and provide insights into where the model's predictions fall short.

Moreover, data analysis is integral to refining prompts in language models. By analyzing data from previous prompts and responses, we can understand what types of prompts yield engaging and relevant responses. This understanding allows us to continually refine our prompts for improved outcomes.

Finally, data analysis helps us spot opportunities for optimization. Through careful examination of the data, we may find ways to improve the efficiency or performance of our AI models, making them faster, more accurate, or more useful.

Overall, data analysis is a critical skill in AI and prompt engineering, enabling us to improve our AI models' performance and usability continually.

For more information about the importance of data analysis in AI, you may refer to the following resources:

Why Data Analysis is Important in AI?
https://towardsdatascience.com/why-data-analysis-is-important-in-ai-f52d472f41c7

Role of data analysis in artificial intelligence
https://www.jigsawacademy.com/blogs/ai-ml/role-of-data-analysis-in-artificial-intelligence/

The Data Analysis Process

Data analysis is a multi-step process that involves several stages, each contributing to the final outcome - the extraction of valuable insights from raw data. Here is a brief overview of each step.

Data Collection

This is the first stage where we gather relevant data for our analysis. The data can come from numerous sources, including databases, online sources, user interactions, or sensors. The quality and relevance of the data collected significantly impact the insights derived later in the process.

Methods of Data Collection in Data Analysis
https://www.mygreatlearning.com/blog/data-collection-methods/

Data Cleaning: Once the data is collected, it is important to clean and preprocess it. This stage involves dealing with missing values, outliers, inconsistencies, and errors that could potentially skew the results of the analysis. It is a crucial step as the quality of the data influences the validity of the insights.

A Complete Guide to Data Cleaning
https://towardsdatascience.com/a-complete-guide-to-data-cleaning-92e5a2e80204

Data Transformation

Here, the cleaned data is manipulated or transformed to prepare it for analysis. This can involve various processes like normalizing data, aggregating data, creating new variables, or converting the data into a different format.

Data Transformation in Data Mining
https://www.geeksforgeeks.org/data-transformation-in-data-

mining/

Data Modelling: In this stage, statistical or machine learning models are applied to the data to identify patterns, relationships, or make predictions. The choice of model depends on the nature of the data and the specific question being asked.

What is Data Modelling? Conceptual, Logical, & Physical Data Models
https://www.guru99.com/data-modelling-conceptual-logical.html

Interpretation and Visualization

Once the data is analyzed, the results are interpreted and often visualized to communicate the findings effectively. This could involve creating charts, graphs, or other visual representations that make the patterns and insights derived from the data easy to understand.

Data Visualization Guide for Beginners
https://chartio.com/learn/dashboards-and-reporting/data-visualization-guide/

Each stage of the data analysis process adds value and brings us closer to the end goal: uncovering valuable insights from the data.

The data analysis process is iterative rather than linear - the insights derived from the data might prompt further questions, leading to additional data collection, cleaning, transformation, and modelling stages.

Through a solid understanding of this process, we can better harness data's power to inform our AI models' design and prompt engineering strategies.

Unveiling Insights: The End Goal of Data Analysis

The end goal of data analysis is not merely to crunch numbers or fill spreadsheets. It's about unveiling insights that were not apparent at the outset. Insights that can shape strategies, inform decisions, and propel innovation.

In the context of AI and prompt engineering, the insights from data analysis play several vital roles:

Evaluating Model Performance

Insights derived from data analysis can help assess how well an AI model is performing. For instance, if an AI chatbot is trained to assist customers, data analysis can reveal whether the chatbot is successfully resolving customer queries, how quickly it does so, and where the bottlenecks are.

Model Evaluation, Model Selection, and Algorithm Selection in Machine Learning
https://arxiv.org/abs/1811.12808

Refining Prompts: Analyzing the data collected from previous prompts and the responses they generated can unveil insights about what works and what doesn't. These insights can guide the process of refining prompts to elicit more engaging, relevant, or accurate responses from AI models.

Prompt Engineering for GPT-3
https://towardsdatascience.com/prompt-engineering-for-gpt-3-5c5ef715db18

Identifying Improvement Areas

Data analysis can highlight areas where the AI model may not be performing up to the mark. This could be certain types of prompts it struggles with, specific topics it doesn't handle well, or particular contexts where its performance dips.

Improving the Interpretability of Deep Learning Models: A Perspective from the Medical Domain

https://journals.plos.org/plosone/article?id=10.1371/
journal.pone.0256256

Supporting Decision Making

The insights derived from data analysis also help in making informed decisions. For example, based on the performance of an AI model in various areas, one can decide where to invest resources for improvement, whether it's worth deploying the model in its current state, and so on.

Decision Making Using Machine Learning: The Case of Reading Incentive
https://pubsonline.informs.org/doi/10.1287/isre.2018.0799

Data analysis serves as the bridge between raw data and meaningful action. By unravelling hidden insights, it empowers us to fine-tune our AI models, make better decisions, and ultimately drive meaningful outcomes in the world of prompt engineering and beyond.

Data Interpretation and Prediction

Interpreting the results of data analysis is a critical skill in the AI domain. The insights derived from your data are only as good as your ability to understand them and put them into action. This process goes beyond simply looking at the numbers; it's about discerning patterns, identifying trends, and making informed predictions about future behaviour based on historical data.

Here are key aspects to consider when interpreting data.

Understanding the Context

The context is vital when interpreting data. It's crucial to understand where the data comes from, what it represents, and the conditions under which it was collected.

Data Context Is as Important as Data Quality
https://www.tdwi.org/articles/2019/12/23/diq-all-data-context-is-as-important-as-data-quality

Recognizing Patterns and Trends: The ability to spot patterns and trends in your data can lead to valuable insights. For example, if you observe that certain types of prompts consistently lead to more engaging responses from an AI model, you might focus on developing similar prompts in the future.

Trend Analysis: A Key Concept in Data Visualization
https://www.tableau.com/learn/articles/trend-analysis

Making Predictions

Predictive analytics is a powerful tool in the AI toolkit. Using historical data, we can forecast future behaviour, anticipate problems before they arise, and identify opportunities for improvement.

Understanding Predictive Analytics
https://www.ibm.com/cloud/learn/predictive-analytics

Considering Uncertainty

It's essential to keep in mind that data analysis often involves dealing with uncertainty. The results should be interpreted as probabilities, not certainties, and it's critical to understand the potential sources of error or bias in your analysis.

Uncertainty in AI systems
https://plato.stanford.edu/entries/uncertainty/

Ultimately, the aim of data interpretation and prediction is to transform the raw output of your data analysis into actionable insights. It's about extracting meaning from the data that you can use to guide your decisions and shape your strategies in prompt engineering and AI development.

Data Analysis as a Tool for Prompt Engineering

In the context of prompt engineering, data analysis is an invaluable tool that can guide us toward better outcomes. It's important to clarify that employing data analysis in prompt engineering does not necessitate becoming a data scientist. Rather, it's about leveraging the power of data to inform your decisions and optimize your results.

Here are a few key ways that data analysis can enhance your prompt engineering efforts.

Performance Evaluation

Data analysis can provide insights into how well your AI model is performing. By analyzing the responses to different prompts, you can understand what's working well and what needs improvement.

How to Measure the Performance of Your AI Model
https://www.dataiku.com/learn/guide/machine-learning/
performance-metrics.html

Prompt Optimization

The responses generated by your AI model can be significantly influenced by the prompts you use. Data analysis can reveal patterns in what kinds of prompts lead to the most engaging or accurate responses, allowing you to refine your approach.

The Art and Science of Prompt Optimization
https://chatbotslife.com/the-art-and-science-of-prompt-
optimization-a4d2f35a8417

Insight Discovery

Beyond performance evaluation and prompt optimization, data

analysis can also uncover unexpected insights. For instance, you might discover that certain types of prompts work particularly well for a specific subset of your user base, leading you to personalize your approach.

Insights from Data Analysis
https://www.kdnuggets.com/2020/05/make-data-analysis-automated-insights.html

Predictive Power

Data analysis can also provide a forward-looking view. By identifying trends in your data, you can make informed predictions about how changes to your prompts might affect the responses from your AI model.

The Power of Predictive Analytics
https://www.sas.com/en_us/insights/analytics/predictive-analytics.html

In essence, data analysis empowers you to make evidence-based decisions in your prompt engineering work. By analyzing the data at your disposal, you can continually refine your approach, ultimately leading to better prompts, more engaging responses, and a more effective AI model.

SECRETS OF THE TRADE: PROMPT ENGINEERING TECHNIQUES

I t's time to dive into the heart of what makes a prompt engineer - the methods, the techniques, and the artistry involved in crafting the perfect prompts and interacting effectively with AI models.

Think of this chapter as a magical grimoire filled with spells, secrets, and enchantments. Here, we unravel the mysteries and the mechanics behind effective prompt crafting, fine-tuning AI responses, managing ambiguous prompts, and evaluating and improving the efficiency of prompts.

This is where you transition from understanding the tools and technologies to actually using them and exploring their potential. It's akin to learning how to paint. At first, you understand the tools - the brushes, the paints, the canvas. But then comes the actual artistry - how to apply each stroke, which colours to mix, what details to highlight - the same goes for prompt engineering.

By the end of this chapter, you won't just know how to 'use' prompts, you'll know how to 'craft' them. You'll not just interact with AI models but learn to 'dance' with them, leading and following as needed. You'll become more than a technician; you'll be a prompt 'artist', creating interactive, engaging, and effective AI experiences.

So, get ready for a thrilling expedition into the heart of prompt engineering! Let's delve into the art of the ask, perfect our dance with AI, juggle the uncertainties of language, and cook up the perfect recipe for successful prompts.

The Art Of The Ask: Crafting Effective Prompts

It's often said that the quality of your life is determined by the quality of the questions you ask. The same holds true for prompt engineering. The quality of your AI interactions is, to a large extent, determined by the quality of the prompts you craft. This is the 'Art of the Ask'.

Crafting effective prompts is like writing a compelling novel. It involves a deep understanding of the context, the characters (users and the AI), and the plot (the goal of the interaction). It's about being precise yet flexible, simple yet comprehensive, and direct yet engaging. It's more than just input; it's a strategic conversation initiator.

To create effective prompts, you need to dive into the heart of your AI, understand its capabilities and limitations, and align this understanding with the needs and expectations of the user. It's like being a translator, facilitating a smooth conversation between a human and an AI.

Throughout this section, we'll explore the essentials of crafting effective prompts. We'll look into their structure, learn to balance specificity and openness, discover how to guide the AI's responses and understand the role of creativity and experimentation in prompt crafting.

By the end of this part, you'll be a master wordsmith, able to craft prompts that evoke engaging, relevant, and precise responses from your AI. It's like learning to compose a beautiful symphony, where every note, every rest, and every rhythm works together to create a masterpiece. So, let's begin our journey into the art of the ask!

Understanding the Context

Here we will explore the importance of understanding the context when crafting prompts. It's crucial to know what the AI can do and how the user interacts with it.

Understanding the AI's Capabilities and Limitations

The first step to effectively crafting prompts is understanding your AI's capabilities and limitations. Each AI model has its strengths, weaknesses, and idiosyncrasies that can be leveraged or navigated to optimize its performance.

AI's Capabilities: Start by familiarizing yourself with the tasks your AI is trained to perform. Is it a chatbot designed for customer service, a language model like GPT-3, or an AI for medical diagnosis? Understanding what the AI has been designed and trained to do will provide a foundation for what kinds of prompts you can construct and the type of responses you can expect.

AI's Limitations: Equally important is knowing what your AI cannot do. No AI is perfect, and understanding its limitations will help you set realistic expectations, avoid potential pitfalls, and craft prompts that steer clear of these limitations. For instance, GPT-3, as of my last training cut-off in 2021, does not have real-time learning or understanding of new information after its training cut-off.

AI's Quirks: Lastly, just like humans, AI systems have their quirks - certain ways they tend to respond or errors they're prone to make. Spending time interacting with the AI and observing its responses will give you a feel for these quirks, which you can account for when crafting prompts.

Understanding the User's Perspective and Expectations

Understanding the user's perspective and expectations is critical for crafting effective prompts. This involves getting to know the needs, preferences, and experience level of the user.

User Needs: Different users have different needs, and it's vital to know what these are. For example, a user querying an AI medical diagnosis system will likely need clear, concise, and accurate information, while a user chatting with a conversational AI may be looking for engaging and natural-sounding responses.

User Preferences: Each user will also have their preferences - their favored mode of interaction, the level of detail they prefer, the tone and style of communication they find most appealing. Tailoring your prompts to these preferences can significantly enhance user engagement and satisfaction.

User Experience Level: Understanding the user's experience level with AI interactions can also inform your prompt crafting. New users might need more guidance and explanatory prompts, while experienced users may prefer more streamlined and direct prompts.

Understanding the Interaction Context

Finally, understanding the context of the interaction is crucial. This involves considering the purpose of the interaction, the environment it takes place in, and the history of interactions (if any).

Interaction Purpose: What is the goal of the AI interaction? Is it to provide information, assist with a task, entertain, or engage in conversation? The purpose of the interaction will heavily influence the structure and content of your prompts.

Interaction Environment: The environment or platform of the interaction can also impact prompt crafting. An AI interaction over a voice assistant may require different prompts than one over a text-based chatbot due to the differences in communication mode.

Interaction History: For AI systems capable of maintaining context over multiple turns or sessions, the history of past interactions can provide valuable context for future prompts. It allows you to build continuity, reference past exchanges, and craft prompts that feel coherent and personalized over time.

By diving deep into these areas of understanding - the AI, the user, and the interaction - you can create prompts that facilitate effective and engaging AI interactions.

The Structure of a Prompt

What is the anatomy of a good prompt? What components make a prompt effective and how do we structure it for optimal responses?

A well-crafted prompt has several key elements that work together to solicit a desirable response from the AI. Understanding these elements can significantly enhance the effectiveness of your prompt crafting:

Clear Intent

The aim or purpose of the prompt must be clear. What do you want the AI to do or understand? Are you asking it a question, instructing it to perform a task, or starting a conversation? Make sure your intent comes through clearly in your prompt.

Specificity

A good prompt is specific enough to guide the AI's response but not so specific that it stifles the AI's capability to generate diverse, creative outputs. It's a delicate balance to maintain. For example, if you're using a language model AI like GPT-3, instead of just asking "Tell me about dogs," you might ask, "Can you provide a brief overview of the main dog breeds in the United States?" The latter is more specific and gives the AI a clearer guideline of what you expect in its response.

Contextual Information

Providing relevant context can help the AI generate a more accurate and relevant response. This could involve setting up the situation, giving background information, or specifying the format you want the response in. For example, if you're asking the AI for a recipe recommendation, providing context like "I'm looking for a quick and easy vegetarian recipe for dinner tonight" will guide the AI to generate a more suitable response.

Natural Language

While AI models can understand and process commands in a wide variety of formats, using natural, conversational language can often lead to more engaging and human-like responses. Make sure your prompts are conversationally appropriate and flow naturally.

Prompt Length

The length of your prompt can also impact its effectiveness. While there's no one-size-fits-all rule, prompts that are too short might lack necessary details, while prompts that are too long might confuse the AI with too much information. Find a balance that includes necessary details but is also concise and to the point.

Feedback Loop

Especially for ongoing interactions or iterative prompt crafting, consider incorporating a feedback loop to learn from previous interactions. This might mean adjusting your prompts based on previous AI responses or user feedback to continually improve the AI's performance.

The structure of your prompt can greatly influence the AI's response. By considering these factors, you can craft prompts that effectively guide your AI towards the desired outputs.

Balancing Specificity and Openness

Striking the right balance between specificity and openness in your prompts is crucial for generating effective AI responses. Each approach has its benefits and potential pitfalls, and understanding these can guide your prompt crafting process.

Specificity in Prompts

Specific prompts provide clear guidelines on what you expect in the AI's response. This can help ensure that the AI's output is relevant and aligned with your needs. For example, instead of saying "Tell me about dogs," you might say "Tell me about the lifespan and characteristics of Border Collies." The latter prompt is more specific and guides the AI to provide the exact information you're looking for.

However, overly specific prompts can also limit the AI's response and stifle its creative potential. If the prompt is too narrow or restrictive, it might prevent the AI from providing additional useful information or exploring different avenues of thought.

Openness in Prompts

On the other hand, open prompts give the AI more freedom to generate diverse and creative responses. These types of prompts can be particularly useful in brainstorming or exploratory situations where you're not looking for one specific answer. An open prompt like "Tell me about dogs" leaves a lot of room for the AI to decide what information to provide.

But while openness can inspire creativity, it can also lead to responses that are off-topic, too broad, or not useful. If a prompt is too open, the AI might not provide the specific information you're looking for.

Striking the Balance

The key to crafting effective prompts is finding the right balance between specificity and openness based on your particular needs. Here are some things to consider:

Purpose of the Interaction

Are you looking for a specific piece of information, or are you brainstorming or exploring a topic? If it's the former, leaning towards specificity might be beneficial. If it's the latter, an open prompt could yield more interesting results.

User Expectations

Consider what the user expects in the AI's response. If they're looking for specific advice or a direct answer, a specific prompt might be better. If they're looking for a range of ideas or a discussion, an open prompt might be more appropriate.

AI Capabilities

Keep in mind the capabilities and limitations of the AI. Some AIs might be better at handling open prompts and generating creative responses, while others might be more suited to specific prompts where they can leverage their knowledge base.

Iteration

Remember that prompt crafting is often an iterative process. You might start with a more open prompt and then gradually add specificity based on the AI's responses and user feedback.

By understanding the impacts of specificity and openness and how to balance them, you can craft prompts that generate the most effective and relevant AI responses.

Guiding AI's Responses

Guiding the AI's responses is an important skill in prompt engineering. By effectively directing the AI, you can obtain more relevant, useful, and engaging responses. However, guiding the AI is a delicate balance. You want to shape the AI's responses without stifling its creative and generative capabilities. Here are some strategies to help you guide the AI's responses:

Utilize Explicit Instructions

One way to guide the AI's response is to provide explicit instructions in your prompts. For example, if you're using AI for a brainstorming session, you might say, "Generate five unique ideas for a new mobile application that encourages healthy eating habits." In this case, the AI knows exactly what you're asking for, which should help guide its response.

Leverage System Level Instructions

Another method is to use system level instructions that guide the AI's behavior across multiple prompts. These instructions can shape the AI's overall behavior, allowing it to better understand and adhere to the goal of the task. For instance, if you're using the AI to generate creative content, a system level instruction could be, "Try to be creative and think outside the box in your responses."

Specify the Format of the Response

You can also guide the AI by specifying the format you want the response in. This can be particularly useful when you need the output in a specific structure. For example, if you want the AI to generate a recipe, your prompt could be, "Provide a recipe for a vegetarian lasagna, including a list of ingredients, quantities, and step-by-step preparation instructions."

Use Clarifying Questions

Sometimes, you can guide the AI by asking clarifying questions. This can help the AI generate a response that is more in line with what you're looking for. For example, if you're discussing a complex topic, you might ask, "Can you explain that in simpler terms?"

Iterative Refinement

Prompt engineering often involves an iterative process where you refine your prompts based on the AI's responses. If the AI's initial response doesn't meet your expectations, you can adjust your prompt, add more details, or provide further guidance to shape its next response.

By using these techniques, you can effectively guide your AI's responses, making your AI interactions more productive and rewarding. Remember, the goal is not to control every aspect of the AI's output, but to guide it in a direction that aligns with your objectives.

Creativity and Experimentation in Prompt Crafting

In the journey of prompt engineering, the destination is important - but so is the journey itself. It's not just about reaching a specific outcome but also about exploring new avenues, trying different approaches, and learning from the process. This is where creativity and experimentation come into play.

Creativity: The Fuel for Prompt Crafting

Creativity in prompt crafting is about thinking outside the box. It involves asking questions in novel ways, rephrasing prompts, using different linguistic techniques, and even playing around with the tone, style, or format of your prompts.

For example, instead of asking the AI, "What is the capital of France?", you could say, "If I were to visit the country famous for its Eiffel Tower and delicious croissants, which city would I find myself in?" The latter prompt is more engaging and could even encourage the AI to provide a more detailed and interesting response.

Creativity is also about understanding the nuances of language and using them to your advantage. The use of metaphors, analogies, humor, and storytelling can make your prompts more effective and engaging.

Experimentation: The Engine of Learning

While creativity fuels your journey, experimentation propels it forward. It's through experimenting with different prompts and observing the AI's responses that we truly learn and improve.

Experimentation might involve varying the complexity of the prompt, altering its structure, or changing its tone. For example, if a direct question isn't yielding the expected response, you could rephrase it as a hypothetical scenario or as an open-ended question.

It's also about being open to failure. Not all experiments will yield positive results, and that's okay. Each failed attempt is a learning opportunity, an insight into the AI's functioning, and a step towards improvement.

Bringing Creativity and Experimentation Together

Creativity and experimentation in prompt crafting are not isolated. They work together, feeding off each other. Your creativity sparks new ideas, and through experimentation, you test these ideas, learn from them, and refine your future prompts.

When you start treating prompt crafting as a creative and experimental process, you'll not only improve your prompts but also make the process more engaging and enjoyable. Remember, prompt engineering isn't a rigid discipline. It's an art form, a space where you can express your creativity, test new ideas, and continually learn and evolve.

The Perfect Dance: Fine-Tuning Your Ai Partner

Working with AI is not a one-way street. It's not about merely feeding it prompts and expecting perfect responses. Instead, it's more of a dance, a synchronized partnership where both you, the prompt engineer, and the AI learn, adapt, and improvise to produce the most harmonious results. Welcome to 'The Perfect Dance'!

Imagine a Tango performance. The lead dancer provides direction, but for the performance to shine, both dancers need to understand each other's movements, adapt to the rhythm, and maintain a seamless connection. In our case, the lead dancer is the prompt engineer, and the AI is the partner.

Fine-tuning AI involves adjusting its parameters to improve its performance - to make it more responsive, accurate, and intuitive. But it goes beyond technical tweaking. It's about understanding how the AI 'thinks', predicting its responses, and shaping its learning process.

In this section, we'll delve into the intricacies of this dance. We'll learn how to guide the AI in its learning, understand its quirks, and refine its performance. We'll unravel how to build an intuitive connection with the AI, predict its responses, and adapt our prompts to achieve the desired results.

By the end of this part, you'll not only know how to fine-tune your

AI partner, but you'll also understand the dance. You'll be able to lead your AI, follow its rhythm, and together, create a captivating performance. So, let's get our dancing shoes on and prepare for a riveting Tango with AI!

Understanding AI's Rhythm

Just like a dance partner, each AI has its rhythm. This rhythm consists of patterns in how the AI responds, the contexts it understands better, the mistakes it tends to make, its speed of processing prompts, and so on. Understanding this rhythm is crucial in developing an effective relationship with the AI, which in turn, significantly improves the quality of its responses.

Deciphering the AI's Patterns

One of the first steps in understanding an AI's rhythm is to recognize its patterns. This could be in the form of the AI's ability to comprehend certain types of prompts better than others or its propensity to generate specific types of responses.

For example, you might notice that the AI often provides more elaborate and relevant responses to open-ended questions compared to yes/no questions. Or perhaps, the AI struggles with understanding metaphors but excels at interpreting literal language.

Recognizing these patterns gives you valuable insights into how to craft your prompts. If the AI responds well to open-ended questions, you might opt to use them more frequently. If it struggles with metaphors, you might decide to use literal language or add additional context when using metaphoric language.

Embracing the AI's Quirks

Just like humans, AI systems have their quirks. These are unique characteristics or tendencies that deviate from the expected behavior. While some might view these quirks as flaws, they can also be seen as opportunities for learning and adaptation.

For instance, you might find that your AI has a penchant for interpreting prompts more literally than intended, or perhaps it tends to offer excessively verbose responses. Instead of viewing these as shortcomings, you can leverage them to refine your prompt crafting. You could add more context to guide the AI's understanding or use directives to limit the length of the response.

Developing Your AI Intuition

As you decipher the AI's patterns and embrace its quirks, you'll start developing an intuition for how the AI thinks and operates. You'll start predicting how the AI might respond to a prompt, or understand why it responded a certain way to a previous prompt.

This intuition, much like understanding the rhythm of a dance partner, is invaluable. It allows you to anticipate and adapt your steps—your prompts—to guide the AI towards the desired outcomes. It helps you transform the interaction from a mechanical process into a harmonious dance.

In summary, understanding the AI's rhythm isn't a one-off task. It's a continuous process of observation, learning, and adaptation. It's about being attuned to the AI's patterns, appreciating its quirks, and developing an intuition for its responses. It's this understanding that forms the foundation for the perfect dance with your AI partner.

Guiding Your AI Partner

Learning to guide your AI partner in its learning process is akin to leading in a dance. You, as the prompt engineer, must provide the right signals (prompts) that help your AI partner understand the context, respond appropriately, and improve over time.

Laying the Groundwork with Clear Context

One of the first steps in guiding your AI partner is to provide clear context through your prompts. Context acts as a compass that guides the AI's understanding and response.

For instance, if you're trying to get the AI to generate a list of pros and cons about a certain topic, instead of merely asking "What are the pros and cons?", provide more context, such as "What are the pros and cons of using electric vehicles over conventional gasoline cars?"

A well-defined context sets the stage for the AI's response, giving it clear boundaries within which to operate, and resulting in a more relevant and precise output.

Using Directives to Shape Responses

Another effective strategy in guiding the AI is the use of directives. Directives are instructions embedded within the prompts that guide the AI on the structure, format, or content of the response.

For example, if you want a concise explanation of a concept, you could include a directive in your prompt like: "Explain quantum physics in a concise and easy-to-understand way for a high school student". The directives here are "concise", "easy-to-understand", and "for a high school student".

Providing Feedback

Feedback is a critical part of guiding your AI. This can take the form of upvotes, downvotes, or text feedback on the AI's responses. Feedback helps the AI learn from its mistakes, understand what it's doing well, and ultimately improve its performance.

Remember, guiding your AI is not about strict control, but gentle guidance. It's about providing clear context, using directives to shape responses, and offering constructive feedback. By leading effectively, you can help your AI partner generate responses that are more relevant, insightful, and engaging, making your dance together a truly captivating performance.

Refining the Dance

While understanding your AI partner's rhythm and guiding it appropriately is part of the fine-tuning process, another crucial aspect is the technical side of things. This is where you, as the lead dancer, adjust the dance steps, refine the choreography, and polish your AI partner's performance. In AI terms, this is done by adjusting various parameters of the AI model to improve its performance, making it more responsive, accurate, and intuitive.

Understanding the Parameters

Fine-tuning an AI model involves adjusting its parameters. These parameters, often called hyperparameters, determine how the model learns. They include learning rate (how quickly the model adapts to new data), batch size (how many data points the model looks at in one go), and many others. Adjusting these parameters can dramatically change the model's performance and behavior.

For instance, a high learning rate might make the model learn quickly, but it can also make it overshoot the optimal solution. On the other hand, a low learning rate might make the model learn slowly but steadily, allowing it to reach a more precise solution.

The Fine-Tuning Process

The process of fine-tuning involves running the AI model with different parameter settings and observing the results. This is typically done through a process known as cross-validation, where the data is split into training and validation sets. The model is trained on the training set with a certain set of parameters, and its performance is evaluated on the validation set.

The aim is to find the set of parameters that gives the best performance on the validation set. This process may be repeated multiple times, iterating over different sets of parameters until the best ones are found.

Evaluating the Performance

Evaluating the performance of an AI model involves measuring how well it performs on certain tasks. There are many different evaluation metrics, depending on the task at hand. For instance, accuracy, precision, recall, and F1 score are commonly used metrics for classification tasks.

By observing these metrics, you can assess how well your model is performing and where it needs improvement. This will help you make informed decisions when adjusting the model's parameters.

Just like a dance performance requires rehearsal, refinement, and critique, the process of fine-tuning your AI partner requires a deep understanding of its parameters, a careful adjustment process, and a thorough evaluation of its performance. Only through this refinement can you ensure a seamless, captivating dance with your AI partner.

Predicting Responses

In our dance metaphor, predicting responses is akin to understanding the moves your dance partner is likely to make based on your lead. For an AI model, this means anticipating the kind of responses a specific prompt might generate. This ability to foresee responses is fundamental to crafting more effective, impactful prompts and to refining the interaction between user and AI.

Grasping the AI's Language Model

Predicting AI responses necessitates a firm grasp of the AI's language model, i.e., how it generates text based on the input it receives. The model isn't merely responding to your prompts; it's using a vast amount of pre-training data to predict what comes next in a sequence of words. It does not understand the text in the way humans do but uses statistical patterns it has learned from the data to generate responses.

By understanding the mechanics of the language model, you can anticipate certain tendencies in the AI's responses. For instance, GPT-3, a model developed by OpenAI, tends to be verbose and overuses certain phrases.

The Role of Experimentation

Experimentation plays a significant role in predicting responses. By providing a variety of prompts and observing the AI's responses, you can start to notice patterns and tendencies, improving your ability to foresee how the AI will react to specific inputs. It's like learning the moves of your dance partner—the more you practice, the better you anticipate their steps.

Impact of Fine-tuning

Fine-tuning can substantially impact an AI's responses. By tweaking certain parameters, you can influence the way the AI responds to prompts. For example, adjusting the "temperature" parameter can make the AI's responses more deterministic or more random. Understanding these parameters can provide more control over the AI's responses, improving your ability to predict them.

By understanding the AI's language model, experimenting with a variety of prompts, and using fine-tuning to influence responses, you can enhance your ability to predict AI responses. It's like developing a deep connection with your dance partner—knowing their tendencies, their quirks, and their style, enabling you to anticipate their next move and guide the dance more effectively.

Adapting to AI

In any dance, both partners must be adaptable, ready to change pace or rhythm as the music demands. The same applies to your relationship with AI. While AI can be extraordinarily precise, it isn't perfect and can sometimes take unexpected turns or make errors. Your ability to adapt, improvise, and learn from these instances is an integral part of becoming a proficient prompt engineer.

Adapting to AI's Inherent Limitations

AI systems, while sophisticated, still have limitations. For example, they lack the ability to comprehend context in the same way humans do, they might overuse certain phrases, or they might produce verbose responses. Adaptability involves understanding these limitations, anticipating possible deviations, and being prepared to correct or adjust your prompts accordingly.

Learning from Mistakes

AI can sometimes generate incorrect or inappropriate responses. Rather than viewing these as failures, treat them as learning opportunities. Analyze why the AI responded the way it did. What aspect of the prompt led to this response? How can the prompt be altered to elicit a more appropriate or accurate response? This iterative learning process is key to adaptability.

Improvisation and Creativity

Adapting to AI also involves a degree of creativity and improvisation. If an AI isn't responding as expected, don't hesitate to think outside the box and experiment with new kinds of prompts. Sometimes, the most innovative solutions come from unforeseen challenges.

Iterative Improvement

Adaptation is an ongoing process. It's about continuously refining your prompts, learning from the AI's responses, and constantly improving your interaction with the AI. Just like in a dance, as you spend more time with your partner, you learn their moves, their rhythms, and how to seamlessly match their steps.

Adapting to AI is about embracing the unexpected, learning from missteps, and being willing to improvise. This adaptability not only makes you a better prompt engineer but also makes your dance with AI a more harmonious and rewarding experience.

Juggling Uncertainty: Managing Ambiguity In Prompts

Welcome to the most intriguing part of our journey, where we venture into the nebulous realm of ambiguity in prompts - 'Juggling Uncertainty'. Language, by its nature, is fluid, flexible, and at times, frustratingly ambiguous. As a prompt engineer, dealing with this ambiguity isn't just a skill, it's an art form.

Picture yourself as a skilled juggler, keeping multiple interpretations in the air as you craft your prompts. Ambiguity might come from the meaning of words, the context of the interaction, or even the intent of the user. Like a juggler, you must manage these uncertainties, ensuring that the core message isn't lost in the chaos.

The Nature of Ambiguity

Ambiguity in language is a pervasive phenomenon that adds a layer of complexity to prompt engineering. Let's delve into understanding its nature, the challenges it presents, and why mastering it can lead to improved AI interactions.

Understanding Ambiguity

At its core, ambiguity refers to the presence of two or more possible meanings within a single sentence or phrase. It's an inherent property of human languages—words and sentences often carry multiple meanings depending on the context they're used in.

For instance, take a simple sentence like "I saw her duck." This could mean you saw a woman ducking to avoid something, or it could mean you saw a woman's duck. The meaning is ambiguous and depends entirely on the context.

Ambiguity in AI and Prompt Engineering

When it comes to interacting with an AI, this ambiguity can lead to unexpected responses. If a prompt can be interpreted in multiple ways, the AI might not understand it in the way the user intended. This can result in an incorrect or irrelevant response, leading to user frustration and a breakdown in communication.

Moreover, ambiguity can also arise from the AI's responses. The AI might generate a response that's open to multiple interpretations, leaving the user confused about its meaning.

Mastering Ambiguity for Improved AI Interactions

While ambiguity presents a challenge, it also provides an opportunity. Mastering ambiguity means becoming adept at crafting prompts that minimize potential confusion and understanding how to handle ambiguous responses from the AI.

Developing this skill involves understanding the context, anticipating possible misinterpretations, and structuring prompts in a way that guides the AI towards the intended interpretation.

Moreover, when the AI produces an ambiguous response, the ability to identify this and reformulate the prompt can significantly improve the quality of the interaction.

In essence, ambiguity is a complex yet fascinating aspect of language. While it adds a layer of complexity to prompt engineering, gaining mastery over it can significantly enhance the effectiveness of your AI interactions. It's part of the 'juggling act' in the world of AI, keeping the conversation on track while handling the fluidity and flexibility of human language.

Identifying Sources of Uncertainty

Effective management of ambiguity starts by identifying its sources. The more familiar we are with where uncertainty originates, the better we can craft our prompts to mitigate it. Let's explore three key sources of ambiguity: word meaning, context, and user intent.

Word Meaning Ambiguity

One common source of ambiguity is in the meaning of words themselves. Many words in the English language have multiple meanings. For instance, the word "bank" can refer to a financial institution, the land alongside a river, or the act of turning an aircraft in flight.

When crafting prompts, it's essential to be aware that certain words might introduce ambiguity. Choosing the most appropriate words and providing sufficient information can help guide the AI towards the correct interpretation.

Contextual Ambiguity

Context plays a significant role in how we interpret language. The same word or sentence can mean different things in different contexts. For instance, "Let's meet at the bank" could mean meeting at a financial institution or by the riverside, depending on the context.

Contextual ambiguity can be challenging in AI interactions as the AI might not have a full understanding of the context. To mitigate this, providing clear and explicit context in your prompts can guide the AI towards a more accurate understanding.

User Intent Ambiguity

Sometimes, ambiguity arises not from the language itself but from the intent of the user. For example, a user might say to an AI assistant, "Set an alarm for 8." But is that 8 AM or 8 PM? The user's intent is unclear, leading to ambiguity.

Identifying potential areas of ambiguous user intent and crafting prompts to clarify such ambiguity can significantly improve the quality of AI interactions.

In summary, understanding the sources of uncertainty—word meaning, context, and user intent—is a fundamental step towards effectively managing ambiguity in prompts. By being aware of these sources, we can craft our prompts more effectively, guiding the AI towards a better understanding and producing more accurate responses.

Strategies for Managing Ambiguity

Managing ambiguity in prompts is both an art and a science. It requires a good understanding of language, intuition, and a fair share of creativity. Here are some practical strategies that can help.

Providing Clear Context

As discussed earlier, context plays a crucial role in how we interpret language. The same sentence can have different meanings depending on the context. Providing clear and explicit context in your prompts can guide the AI towards a more accurate understanding. For example, instead of saying "Send him the report," a more contextual prompt could be "Send the monthly sales report to John."

Clarifying Intent

If a user's intent is ambiguous, it's essential to prompt for clarification rather than making an assumption. For example, if a user says, "Set an alarm for 8," the AI could respond with, "Sure, would you like the alarm to be set for 8 AM or 8 PM?" This allows the AI to clarify the user's intent and respond accurately.

Using Confirmations

Confirmation is another useful strategy to manage ambiguity. For instance, if a user asks the AI to "Book a flight to Paris," the AI could confirm by saying, "Just to confirm, you'd like me to book a flight to Paris, France, correct?" This ensures that the AI understood the user's request correctly before executing the task.

Managing Exceptions

Sometimes, despite our best efforts, the AI might still misinterpret an ambiguous prompt. In such cases, it's important to have a plan for managing these exceptions. This could involve providing the user with an easy way to correct the AI or to start over the conversation.

Remember, managing ambiguity is not about eliminating it—it's about learning how to juggle it effectively. With these strategies in your toolkit, you'll be well-equipped to handle the uncertainties that come with crafting prompts and improve the quality of your AI interactions.

Case Studies: Dissecting Ambiguous Prompts

Learning from real-world examples is a great way to understand and master the art of managing ambiguity. Let's take a closer look at two ambiguous prompts, dissect them, and learn from their outcomes.

Case Study 1: The Double-Edged Sword of Pronouns

Consider a user prompt: "Ask her to send it to me." While it may seem clear to the user, the AI might struggle with this prompt. The ambiguity arises from the pronouns "her" and "it" - the AI doesn't have the context to understand who "her" is and what "it" refers to.

Outcome: Without the necessary context, the AI might ask for clarification or make an inaccurate assumption, leading to an ineffective response.

Lesson: Always aim to provide clear and explicit context, especially when using pronouns. Instead of "Ask her to send it to me," a more specific prompt could be "Ask Alexa to send the meeting notes to me."

Case Study 2: The Challenge of Homonyms

Homonyms are words that are spelled or pronounced the same way but have different meanings. Consider a user prompt: "I want to meet the band." The word "band" is a homonym that could refer to a musical group or a range of frequencies in communications.

Outcome: The AI might incorrectly interpret the user's request depending on its previous learning or the context it has been trained on.

Lesson: When working with homonyms, aim to provide as much context as possible. If the AI is likely to encounter a lot of homonyms in its use case, consider strategies like confirmation or clarification to ensure the right interpretation.

These case studies highlight the challenges and solutions in managing ambiguous prompts. By learning from these real-life examples, you can better understand the intricacies of managing ambiguity and craft more effective prompts.

Mastering the Art of Juggling Uncertainty

The journey through ambiguity is challenging, intriguing, and ultimately rewarding. The skills of identifying the sources of uncertainty, strategizing effective ways to manage them, and learning from real-world examples are all parts of this fascinating journey. Like juggling, the more you practice managing ambiguity, the more skilled you become, and the easier it becomes to keep all the balls in the air.

Continuous Learning

Ambiguity in language is dynamic. New words, phrases, and slang are continuously added to our lexicon, and existing ones evolve. To stay on top of this, you need to cultivate a habit of continuous learning. Regularly expose yourself to different types of language contexts - books, articles, podcasts, social media posts, etc. This will help you understand and adapt to the changing landscape of language ambiguity.

Embrace Uncertainty

Instead of seeing ambiguity as a hurdle, view it as a challenge to overcome. Each ambiguous prompt is a riddle waiting to be solved, a puzzle begging to be pieced together. Embrace this uncertainty, dive into it headfirst, and enjoy the process of finding clarity in chaos.

Practice Makes Perfect

Just as a juggler gets better with practice, you too will become more adept at handling ambiguity the more you do it. Keep crafting prompts, keep experimenting, and keep learning. The more prompts you create, the better you will understand how to guide the AI and manage ambiguity effectively.

Patience and Persistence

The journey to mastering ambiguity isn't a sprint; it's a marathon. It requires patience to understand and untangle the intricate web of language, and persistence to keep going, even when it's challenging. But the rewards, in terms of more effective and engaging AI interactions, are well worth the effort.

By mastering the art of juggling uncertainty, you will not just become a more effective prompt engineer, but also a more creative and critical thinker. So, let's keep juggling, keep learning, and keep refining our art of managing ambiguity in prompts!

The Recipe For Success: Assessing And Improving Your Prompts

As we approach the end of this chapter, it's time to blend all the flavours we've explored into a delicious dish – a successful prompt. This section, 'The Recipe for Success', is where we learn to assess and improve our prompts, continuously refine our techniques and strive for excellence.

Imagine yourself as a master chef. Crafting effective prompts is your recipe, your AI model is the oven, and the responses you get are your culinary creations. As with any recipe, continuous tasting, adjusting, and perfecting is key to a delightful result.

Assessing your prompts involves analyzing AI responses, user feedback, and performance metrics to understand the effectiveness of your prompts. It's about finding the right mix of ingredients: clear instructions, appropriate context, and the right level of specificity. Improving your prompts, on the other hand, involves iterating, experimenting, and learning from your assessments.

The Importance of Data Analysis in AI

The fuel that powers the engines of artificial intelligence is data. From teaching an AI model to recognize speech patterns to understanding the intricacies of natural language, data is the bedrock on which these capabilities are built. Consequently, data analysis emerges as a critical process in AI, including in the realm of prompt engineering.

Data analysis helps us understand the information at our disposal. It allows us to dig into the raw data, sift through it, and uncover patterns and insights that we can leverage. Think of it as the process of extracting diamonds from the rough—only the diamonds are insights, and the rough is raw, unprocessed data.

In the context of AI, data analysis serves two main functions. First, it informs the creation and training of AI models. We use it to understand what kind of data we have, identify patterns, and translate these insights into a format that an AI can learn from. Secondly, it's a critical part of evaluating the performance of our AI models. By analyzing the output of our models and comparing it to our expected results, we can gauge how well the model is doing and where it needs improvement.

In prompt engineering, the role of data analysis is equally significant. Analyzing the responses to different prompts can reveal which prompts produce the most engaging and useful responses. This analysis can guide the process of refining and improving prompts, leading to better user experiences and more effective AI interactions.

But to make any sense of this data, we need to become proficient in the art of data analysis. As we progress through this chapter, we will develop a clearer understanding of this process and its invaluable contribution to AI and prompt engineering.

For further reading, you may want to consider the book "Data Science for Business: What You Need to Know about Data Mining and Data-Analytic Thinking" by Foster Provost and Tom Fawcett. This book offers a deep dive into understanding the importance and impact of data in the field of AI.

Data Science for Business
https://www.amazon.com/Data-Science-Business-data-analytic-thinking/dp/1449361323

The Data Analysis Process

Data analysis is a multifaceted process, involving several distinct but interconnected steps. These steps transform raw, unprocessed data into insightful information that we can use to make informed decisions and drive actions. Although the specific steps can vary based on the data and the particular situation, a general data analysis process includes the following stages.

Data Collection
This is the first step in the process, where we gather data relevant to our question or problem. The data can come from various sources, such as databases, online sources, sensors, or user interactions. The quality and appropriateness of the collected data have a significant impact on the final outcome of the analysis.

Data Cleaning
Once we've collected the data, the next step is to clean it. This involves dealing with missing or inconsistent data and removing any errors or inaccuracies that could skew our analysis. This is a crucial step because the quality of our data influences the quality of our insights.

Data Transformation
In this step, we manipulate the data to prepare it for analysis. This could involve aggregating the data, creating new variables, or converting the data into a different format.

Data Modelling

Here, we apply statistical or machine learning models to our data to uncover patterns, make predictions, or discover relationships among data elements.

Interpretation and Visualization

After analyzing the data, we interpret the results and often visualize them in an understandable and accessible way. This could involve creating charts, graphs, or other visual representations to help make sense of the results.

Each of these steps plays a critical role in turning raw data into actionable insights. As we delve deeper into data analysis, we'll look at each of these steps in more detail and explore how they contribute to our understanding of AI and prompt engineering.

For a comprehensive understanding of the data analysis process, "Python for Data Analysis: Data Wrangling with Pandas, NumPy, and IPython" by Wes McKinney is a great resource. It offers a deep understanding of the data analysis process with practical examples in Python.

Python for Data Analysis
https://www.amazon.com/Python-Data-Analysis-Wrangling-IPython/dp/1491957662

So let's look at each of these stages in more detail.

Data Collection

Data collection is where our data analysis journey begins. It's akin to setting out on an expedition, where the data we gather is like the supplies we'll need for the journey ahead. The goal of this stage is to gather high-quality, relevant data that will answer our questions or solve our problems.

The data we collect can come from a variety of sources. Here are a few examples:

Databases

Structured repositories of data, like SQL databases, are a common source of data. They often contain valuable information about user interactions, transactions, and other key business data.

Online Sources

The internet is a treasure trove of data. We can collect data from websites (through a process called web scraping), APIs (which allow us to access certain data from a service), or online data platforms.

Sensors

In many fields, especially in the Internet of Things (IoT) domain, data from sensors, like temperature sensors, motion sensors, or accelerometers, provide valuable real-time insights.

User Interactions

For many applications, especially in AI, data about how users interact with an application or a website is incredibly valuable. This could be collected through logs, surveys, or through tracking user interactions.

The key to effective data collection is ensuring that the data we collect is relevant to our question and is of high quality. Poor quality data, or data that doesn't actually address our questions, can lead us to incorrect conclusions and ineffective actions.

For an in-depth understanding of the data collection process and the techniques used, you can refer to the book "Data Collection: Planning for and Collecting All Types of Data" by Patricia Pulliam Phillips. It covers all aspects of data collection, from planning to execution, ensuring that you have a comprehensive understanding of this crucial step in the data analysis process.

Data Collection: Planning for and Collecting All Types of Data https://www.amazon.com/Data-Collection-Planning-Collecting-Types/dp/0787982761

Data Cleaning

Just as you would wash and prepare your ingredients before cooking, data cleaning is the process of "preparing" your data before analysis. It's about dealing with the messy aspects of data that can distort our analysis and lead us astray.

Data cleaning, also known as data cleansing or data scrubbing, involves several key steps.

Handling Missing Data

Not all data is complete. We may have missing values for some fields. Depending on the nature of the data and the missing information, we may choose to impute the missing values (i.e., fill in with a calculated value), or we may choose to ignore those data points altogether.

Correcting Inconsistencies

Data, especially when coming from multiple sources, can be inconsistent. For instance, one source may list dates in the MM-DD-YYYY format, while another uses DD-MM-YYYY. We'll need to standardize this data.

Removing Errors or Outliers

Sometimes, data may have errors - values that are clearly incorrect or atypical. These could be due to mistakes in data entry or collection, or they could represent rare events. Depending on the nature of the analysis, we might want to correct or exclude these values.

The goal of data cleaning is to improve the quality of the data we're working with. The old adage "garbage in, garbage out" holds particularly true in data analysis. If our data is full of errors and inconsistencies, our analysis will be unreliable.

For more detailed insights into data cleaning, the book "Data Cleaning" by Ihab Ilyas and Xu Chu offers a comprehensive guide on the methodologies and techniques used to clean data, highlighting why this process is a crucial step in the data analysis pipeline.

Data Cleaning
https://www.amazon.com/Data-Cleaning-Ihab-Ilyas/

dp/1681735830

Data Transformation

After cleaning the data, the next step in the data analysis process is data transformation. This is like a chef preparing and seasoning ingredients before cooking. For data, this "seasoning" might involve aggregating the data, creating new variables, or converting the data into a different format that's more suitable for analysis.

Here are some common data transformation techniques.

Aggregation

This involves summarizing or grouping data. For example, you might aggregate sales data by region to analyze regional trends.

Derivation

This involves creating new variables from existing ones. For instance, if you have data on a person's height and weight, you might derive a new variable: body mass index (BMI).

Conversion

This involves changing the format of data. For example, you might convert a continuous variable (like age) into categories (like age groups).

Data transformation is about shaping and refining your data until it's in the best possible format for analysis. It's another step towards ensuring that your data gives you meaningful, reliable insights.

For an in-depth exploration of data transformation techniques, "Data Wrangling with Python" by Jacqueline Kazil and Katharine Jarmul provides practical examples and methods for transforming and manipulating data. This book is an excellent resource for anyone looking to gain hands-on experience with data transformation.

Data Wrangling with Python
https://www.amazon.com/Data-Wrangling-Python-Tools-

Easier/dp/1491948817

Data Modelling

After transforming the data, we arrive at one of the most exciting stages of the data analysis process: data modelling. This is where we put on our detective hats and dive into the heart of the data. It's here that we aim to uncover patterns, make predictions, or discover relationships among data elements.

Data modelling is about asking questions of your data and applying statistical or machine learning models to seek answers. Here are a few types of data modelling techniques:

Descriptive Models

These models are used to understand and summarize the features of our dataset. They can help describe relationships between variables or outline the structure of the dataset.

Predictive Models

These models make predictions about unseen or future data based on what the model has learned from the training data. Examples include regression models for predicting a continuous outcome or classification models for predicting a categorical outcome.

Prescriptive Models

These models not only predict the future but also suggest actions to benefit from the prediction. They are used in decision-making and optimization problems.

Remember, the goal of data modelling is not necessarily to build the most complex model, but rather to build a model that best answers your specific question or problem with the least complexity.

For further reading on the subject, "The Hundred-Page Machine Learning Book" by Andriy Burkov provides a concise and practical introduction to the fundamentals of machine learning, including various types of data modelling.

The Hundred-Page Machine Learning Book

https://www.amazon.com/Hundred-Page-Machine-Learning-Book/dp/199957950X

Interpretation and Visualization

The final step of the data analysis process is interpreting the results and visualizing them in a way that's understandable and accessible. The aim here is not just to understand what the data is saying, but also to communicate those findings effectively. This step involves explaining the significance of the data in a way that can be easily understood, often by using visual aids like charts, graphs, or diagrams.

Interpretation is about understanding the story the data is telling us. It's about moving beyond raw numbers to meaningful insights. For example, if we were using a regression model to predict user engagement based on prompt length, we might interpret the model's coefficients to understand how changes in prompt length impact engagement.

Visualization, on the other hand, is a powerful way to explore data, uncover insights, and communicate findings. Effective visualizations can highlight trends, reveal patterns, and provide an intuitive understanding of complex data sets. Common visualization tools include bar graphs, scatter plots, line charts, and heat maps.

Keep in mind, the best visualization technique will depend on your specific data and the story you want to tell. It's always important to consider your audience and what visualizations will be most effective in conveying your findings to them.

For further reading, "The Visual Display of Quantitative Information" by Edward R. Tufte is a classic book on the art and science of data visualization.

The Visual Display of Quantitative Information
https://www.amazon.com/Visual-Display-Quantitative-Information/dp/0961392142

Unveiling Insights

Data analysis is a powerful tool for unearthing insights that might otherwise remain hidden. Once you've collected, cleaned, transformed, and modelled your data, the next step is to use that data to answer important questions.

For instance, in the context of prompt engineering, you might use data analysis to evaluate the performance of your model. You could examine response length, coherence, relevance, and other factors to see how well your model is functioning. From there, you can make adjustments and improvements as needed.

You might also use data analysis to find out what types of prompts lead to the most engaging responses. Are shorter prompts more effective? Do users respond better to prompts that ask questions, or ones that make statements? With data analysis, you can answer these questions and more.

Additionally, data analysis can reveal areas where there's room for optimization and improvement. Maybe there are certain types of prompts that your model struggles with, or maybe there's a way to make your prompts even more engaging.

The insights you gain through data analysis aren't just informative—they're actionable. They give you the knowledge you need to improve your model and prompts, leading to better user experiences and more effective AI.

For further exploration into practical applications of data analysis, "Data Science for Business: What You Need to Know about Data Mining and Data-Analytic Thinking" by Foster Provost and Tom Fawcett is a great resource.

Data Science for Business: What You Need to Know about Data Mining and Data-Analytic Thinking
https://www.amazon.com/Data-Science-Business-data-analytic-thinking/dp/1449361323

Data Interpretation and Prediction

Interpreting the results of data analysis involves taking the raw output of your data model - typically a collection of statistics, patterns, and relationships - and making sense of it. This usually requires a good understanding of the context in which the data exists.

For example, in prompt engineering, if you've analyzed your data and found that shorter prompts lead to more engaging responses, you need to interpret this finding. Does it mean that users prefer shorter prompts? Or could it be that shorter prompts are more effective because they're more direct and easier to understand? Interpretation involves understanding what your findings mean in practical terms.

Spotting trends in your data is another essential part of data interpretation. In our example, if you see that the engagement rate has been gradually increasing as your prompts get shorter, that's a trend. Trends are important because they can help you anticipate future behaviour. If you know that shorter prompts have been more effective in the past, you can reasonably predict that they will continue to be more effective in the future.

Making predictions based on your data is called predictive analysis. It involves using your data to make informed guesses about future outcomes. Predictive analysis can be incredibly useful in many fields, including prompt engineering. For example, you might use predictive analysis to estimate how well a new type of prompt will perform based on how similar prompts have performed in the past.

For more on data interpretation and prediction, you may consider reading "The Signal and the Noise: Why So Many Predictions Fail - But Some Don't" by Nate Silver. This book discusses the art and science of prediction in the context of real-world applications.

The Signal and the Noise: Why So Many Predictions Fail - But Some Don't
https://www.amazon.com/Signal-Noise-Many-Predictions-Fail-but/dp/0143125087

Data Analysis as a Tool for Prompt Engineering

As we've journeyed through the process of data analysis, it's crucial to remember that our goal isn't to become data scientists. Instead, we aim to wield the power of data analysis as a potent tool in our prompt engineering toolkit.

Understanding how to collect, clean, transform, model, interpret, and visualize data allows us to optimize our AI models and prompts effectively. It offers us a means to understand the 'why' and 'how' behind the performance of our models. If a certain prompt is eliciting fantastic responses, data analysis helps us uncover the reasons and apply these insights to craft more effective prompts.

Moreover, it aids us in anticipating future outcomes. Once we spot trends and patterns in our data, we can make informed predictions about how alterations in our prompts might influence the AI's responses. This ability to forecast is particularly valuable in constantly evolving fields like AI, enabling us to stay one step ahead.

In short, data analysis is less about the raw numbers and more about the insights those numbers can provide. It's about taking these insights and using them to fuel our prompt engineering efforts, ultimately resulting in AI models that generate better, more engaging responses.

For further reading on using data analysis in practical scenarios, "Data Science for Business: What You Need to Know about Data Mining and Data-Analytic Thinking" by Foster Provost and Tom Fawcett offers a great overview.

Data Science for Business: What You Need to Know about Data Mining and Data-Analytic Thinking
https://www.amazon.com/Data-Science-Business-data-analytic-thinking/dp/1449361323

CASE STUDIES IN PROMPT ENGINEERING

A s we journey further into the captivating world of prompt engineering, it's time to venture out of the theoretical landscape and plunge into the real world. Welcome to Chapter IV: 'Case Studies in Prompt Engineering'. Here, we'll trade the chalkboard for the field, and the blueprints for the architecture, as we analyze real-world applications and scenarios.

This chapter is the 'hands-on' part of your journey. Think of it as a grand museum tour, where each case study is a masterpiece crafted by prompt engineers around the world. We'll stand before each exhibit, marvelling at its brilliance, dissecting its intricacies, and drawing inspiration from its creation.

From businesses harnessing AI to streamline their operations, to educators leveraging it for personalized learning; from customer service chatbots to interactive voice assistants, we'll explore a spectrum of applications. We'll study their prompts, analyze their strategies, and understand their outcomes. We'll learn not only from their triumphs but also from their challenges and failures.

By the end of this chapter, you'll have a comprehensive understanding of prompt engineering in action. You'll learn how to adapt theoretical knowledge to practical situations, understand different strategies for diverse scenarios, and be better equipped to tackle real-world challenges.

So, let's roll up our sleeves and delve into the engaging world of case studies. Let's learn from the past, understand the present, and shape the future of prompt engineering!

Victorious Tales: Success Stories In Prompt Engineering

Welcome to our first exhibit – the hall of fame, showcasing 'Victorious Tales: Success Stories in Prompt Engineering'. In this section, we will celebrate the achievements of prompt engineers who have used their skills to create remarkable solutions, highlighting the potential of what we can achieve.

Think of this as a stroll down a grand gallery of prompt engineering masterpieces, each one a testament to the power of effective prompts and finely-tuned AI. Each tale is a rich tapestry of trials, triumphs, creativity, and innovation.

We'll begin our journey with stories of how well-crafted prompts have transformed businesses, improved customer experiences, and even made breakthroughs in scientific research. We'll dive deep into how these engineers approached their tasks, the strategies they employed, and the results they achieved.

We'll also understand the impacts of these successful prompts, not just on the AI's performance but also on user engagement, satisfaction, and overall business outcomes. And as we explore each tale, we'll distil key lessons, strategies, and best practices that we can apply in our journey as prompt engineers.

So, let's bask in the glory of these victorious tales, drawing inspiration and learning from the best in the world of prompt engineering!

Alright, let's dive into some fascinating stories of success in prompt engineering.

The Savvy Retailer

An online retailer was struggling with a high volume of customer queries regarding product details, delivery times, and returns policy. They introduced a chatbot, trained using well-crafted prompts. The result was a significant reduction in customer service response time, a boost in customer satisfaction, and freeing up human resources for more complex tasks. The prompt engineers made this possible by carefully creating prompts that covered a wide array of common customer questions, all while maintaining a friendly, brand-consistent tone.

The Innovative Research Institute

A research institute used prompt engineering to develop an AI model that could analyze vast amounts of scientific literature for specific information, a task that would take humans an exorbitant amount of time. By using precise, carefully crafted prompts, the AI model was able to extract relevant information efficiently and accurately, aiding in several breakthrough discoveries. This is a testament to how powerful a well-engineered prompt can be when paired with a robust AI model.

The E-Learning Platform

An e-learning platform wanted to personalize its content to cater to each student's unique learning style. Using a mixture of open-ended and specific prompts, they were able to create a dynamic AI tutor that adapted to each student's learning pace and style. This led to improved student engagement and learning outcomes, demonstrating how prompt engineering can personalize and improve user experiences.

These stories underline the importance of thoughtful prompt

engineering and its potential to make a significant difference across various sectors. They showcase how creativity, strategic thinking, and a deep understanding of AI language models can lead to innovative solutions and remarkable success.

Let's delve into some more extreme, transformative examples of prompt engineering.

Transforming Public Health

In a bid to provide widespread, reliable, and instantaneous health information, a public health organization utilized AI and prompt engineering. They developed a chatbot that could answer an array of health-related queries, from symptoms to treatment suggestions. With meticulously engineered prompts, the chatbot could understand diverse health-related inquiries, provide accurate information, and guide users to seek professional medical help when needed. The result was a massive reduction in misinformation and a significant boost in public health education.

Revolutionizing Disaster Response

In the face of natural disasters, prompt responses are critical. An international disaster response agency integrated an AI model into their systems, using finely-crafted prompts to facilitate quick information extraction. This model could sift through countless social media posts and news reports, identify urgent situations, and direct resources effectively. The prompt engineers had to ensure the AI model could understand the severity and urgency of the tone and context of the text. This revolutionary use of prompt engineering resulted in faster response times and more lives saved.

Pioneering Space Exploration

A space exploration agency successfully utilized AI and prompt engineering in its Mars rover mission. The AI model, trained with a series of prompts, could analyze the images sent back by the rover and classify geological formations. The prompt engineering involved was incredibly complex, involving not just language, but also the interpretation of visual data. The success of the mission offered a testament to how far the boundaries of prompt engineering could be pushed.

These extreme cases highlight the extraordinary potential of prompt engineering. They showcase how well-crafted prompts, combined with robust AI models, can address complex, high-stakes challenges, leading to groundbreaking achievements and transforming entire fields.

let's explore some examples of situations where a beginning prompt engineer could make a significant impact in a business setting.

Customer Service Enhancement

Many businesses use customer service chatbots to handle common queries. As a beginning prompt engineer, you could work on improving these chatbots by fine-tuning their prompts. For example, you might make the chatbot's responses sound more human-like or ensure it provides more accurate information. By making these improvements, you could help increase customer satisfaction and reduce the workload of customer service representatives.

Internal Communication

Businesses often use AI tools for internal communication, like scheduling meetings or managing tasks. You could improve these tools by crafting more effective prompts. This might involve making the tool more user-friendly, or it could involve adding new functionalities, like the ability to understand and respond to more complex queries.

Content Creation

AI can help businesses generate content, such as blog posts, social media updates, or product descriptions. As a prompt engineer, you could work on improving the quality of this content. This might involve creating prompts that guide the AI to write in a particular style or to include certain types of information. Your work could help the business create high-quality content more efficiently.

Data Analysis

Businesses often use AI to analyze data, like sales figures or customer feedback. Your role as a prompt engineer could involve improving the accuracy and usefulness of these analyses. For instance, you could create prompts that guide the AI to highlight particularly important pieces of information or to present its findings in a more understandable way.

These are just a few examples of the types of projects you might work on as a beginning prompt engineer in a business setting. Remember, the key to success in these roles is to understand both the technical aspects of AI and the needs of the business.

Learning From Our Ouch Moments: Lessons From Failed Projects

Let's be honest, not every prompt engineering project goes off without a hitch. In our pursuit to create better, more efficient AI models, we will inevitably encounter bumps and even gaping potholes along the way. Welcome to our 'Ouch Moments' - a collection of tales from failed projects. But don't fret! These are not mere stories of failure; they're opportunities to learn, adapt, and innovate. In this chapter, we'll explore what went wrong, why it did, and most importantly, what we can learn from these experiences.

The Overambitious Chatbot

A company decided to develop a customer service chatbot designed to handle all customer queries. The prompt engineers created a range of prompts, but they were far too broad and ambiguous. The chatbot struggled with understanding customer queries, leading to frustration and a loss of customer confidence. The lesson? Trying to create a 'one-size-fits-all' solution can backfire. Instead, it's important to focus on creating specific, clear prompts that can handle a targeted set of queries effectively.

Lost in Translation

A global company aimed to create a multilingual AI model to handle customer interactions across different regions. However, they underestimated the nuances and complexities of languages. The prompts, while effective in English, didn't translate well into other languages. This led to miscommunication, confusing outputs, and a poor user experience. What can we learn? Always take into account the complexity and nuance of language when crafting prompts for multilingual AI models.

The Unpredictable AI Tutor

An e-learning platform wanted to create an AI tutor that could adapt to each student's learning style. They worked tirelessly on complex prompts to cover various learning styles and subjects. However, without clear guidelines and boundaries, the AI often produced unpredictable and irrelevant responses. The takeaway? While it's crucial to allow AI the freedom to adapt, clear boundaries and guidelines need to be established in the prompts to prevent off-track responses.

Data Disaster

A business wanted to use AI to analyze complex data and predict future trends. They spent a lot of time crafting elaborate prompts for their AI model. But the model's responses were often inaccurate or irrelevant. Upon review, they found that their data was inconsistent and of poor quality. The AI was only as good as the data it was trained on. The moral? Quality data is crucial. No matter how good the prompts are, the AI model's effectiveness is limited by the quality of the data it's trained on.

In the world of prompt engineering, failure isn't a setback; it's a stepping stone towards better understanding and improvement. Each 'Ouch Moment' brings with it valuable lessons and insights that make us better equipped to navigate the challenges of the AI landscape. Remember, every great success is built on the foundation of lessons learned from failure. So, let's embrace these moments, learn from them, and move forward in our exciting journey of prompt engineering.

The importance of precision and accuracy cannot be overstated when it comes to medical and safety applications. The margin for error is extremely narrow, and missteps can have severe consequences. Here, we delve into some instances where things didn't go as planned in these critical domains, but also the invaluable lessons learned from these situations.

The Misdiagnosing AI Doctor

A healthcare startup developed an AI model aimed at diagnosing diseases based on patient symptoms and medical history. However, due to an insufficient range of prompts and overreliance on certain symptom combinations, the model ended up misdiagnosing several cases. Some patients were incorrectly reassured, while others were alarmed by false positives. The incident highlighted the need for diverse, well-balanced prompts and continuous monitoring and validation of AI predictions in healthcare.

The Silent Safety Monitor

A manufacturing company introduced an AI system to monitor safety conditions and alert employees to potential hazards. The system was designed with prompts aimed at recognizing a set of predefined risk situations. Unfortunately, the AI failed to alert us about an unusual hazard that did not fit the predefined situations, leading to an avoidable accident. This incident underscored the importance of designing prompts that allow AI to recognize and adapt to new, unexpected situations, especially in safety-critical applications.

The Negligent Drug Interaction Checker

An AI was developed to predict potential drug interactions, aimed at aiding physicians in prescription decisions. Due to poorly designed prompts and lack of specificity, the AI model overlooked several crucial drug interactions, potentially endangering patients' health. This failure taught a valuable lesson about the importance of specificity, precision, and comprehensive domain knowledge when designing prompts for healthcare applications.

The False Alarm System

A security company deployed an AI model to detect and report suspicious activities. However, the prompts designed were not well-calibrated, leading to numerous false alarms. This resulted in wasted resources, frustration, and decreased trust in the system. It served as a potent reminder that prompt calibration is critical for striking the balance between sensitivity and specificity in alert-generating systems.

These cautionary tales remind us of the critical role prompt engineering plays in sensitive domains like healthcare and safety. The failures stress the need for meticulous prompt design, rigorous testing, continuous monitoring, and constant improvements, especially when stakes are high. They illustrate that with great power comes great responsibility. As prompt engineers, we must always be aware of the potential impact of our work and strive for the highest standards of accuracy, reliability, and ethics.

Beginner's Bloopers: Typical Pitfalls And How To Dodge Them

Embarking on your journey as a prompt engineer, you're bound to face some stumbling blocks. However, these hiccups are an essential part of the learning process. Here, we'll highlight common pitfalls for beginners in prompt engineering, how you can learn from them, and strategies to preemptively address potential issues.

Overly Broad Prompts

One of the common missteps beginners make is crafting overly broad prompts. This can lead to vague or irrelevant responses from the AI. To avoid this, aim for specificity. Define your prompt's purpose clearly and ensure it directs the AI towards generating the desired output.

Ignoring Context

Ignoring the context can result in prompts that don't align with the AI model's understanding or knowledge base. To tackle this, familiarize yourself with the model's training data and capabilities. This will help you tailor your prompts better.

Overlooking User Perspective

It's easy to forget that the ultimate recipient of the AI's response is a user. To avoid creating prompts that result in responses that are technically correct but not user-friendly, always consider the user's perspective and needs when crafting prompts.

Lack of Iteration and Testing

Prompts are not a 'set it and forget it' affair. They require regular testing and refinement. Skipping this step could lead to underperforming prompts. Ensure that you have a robust feedback loop and make necessary adjustments based on the AI's performance.

Forgetting about Edge Cases

While it's natural to focus on the most common scenarios, ignoring edge cases can lead to significant issues. When writing prompts, consider uncommon but possible scenarios that might trip up your AI.

Failure, they say, is the best teacher. As a prompt engineer, you will make mistakes – but the key lies in learning from them. Use these mistakes as opportunities for growth. Defensive prompt writing is about anticipating potential issues and addressing them preemptively in your prompts. It's a combination of careful consideration, thorough testing, constant learning, and continuous improvement.

As you navigate through the fascinating world of prompt engineering, remember that every stumble is a step forward. Each mistake you make, and each 'ouch' moment, brings you one step closer to mastering this craft. So, gear up, embrace the challenges, and let's make some magic with AI!

THE FUTURE OF PROMPT ENGINEERING

As we venture into the depths of the thrilling world of AI and language models, it's natural to cast our gaze forward and imagine the possibilities. Just as science fiction has often foreshadowed technological advancements, we too can dream about where prompt engineering may lead us. This chapter, dear reader, is an exploration of the exciting, perhaps even bewildering, frontier of our profession. We'll venture beyond the 'now', and venture into the fascinating realm of tomorrow.

We'll contemplate, predict, and hypothesize about the advancements in the field. We'll analyze trends, gaze into our crystal ball, and even do a bit of fortune-telling. Will our future selves be designing prompts for sentient AIs, or will we be teaching intergalactic languages to our language models? Will we evolve from engineers to diplomats, crafting prompts for peaceful AI-human coexistence?

Let's journey together into the future, and let's imagine what it holds for prompt engineering. We'll explore how technological advancements, research breakthroughs, and shifts in societal understanding could shape our profession. Will prompt engineering remain as it is, or will it transform into something we can scarcely imagine today?

So buckle up, fellow adventurer! Let's head towards the exciting horizon and dare to dream about the future of prompt engineering. It's going to be a wild, exciting ride!

The Next Frontier: Upcoming Trends In Prompt Engineering

As we hover on the cusp of thrilling advancements in artificial intelligence, it's an opportune moment to peek into the crystal ball and consider the trends that are expected to shape the landscape of prompt engineering.

Increasing Personalization

With growing volumes of data and the ability of AI to understand and cater to individual needs, we foresee an increase in personalized prompts. These could facilitate hyper-personalized responses from AI models, resulting in more interactive, tailored user experiences.

Cross-Domain Applications

As AI continues to penetrate various sectors, from healthcare to e-commerce, we anticipate a surge in the need for specialized prompts for diverse domains. Prompt engineers may soon find themselves crafting prompts for AI doctors, virtual shopping assistants, or even AI-powered tutors.

Multi-modal Prompts

As technology evolves, we can expect to see prompts go beyond text. Multi-modal prompts, integrating images, audio, or video, could become commonplace, pushing the boundaries of how we interact with AI models.

AI-Generated Prompts

The future might even see AI models assisting in generating their own prompts. AI could identify gaps in its own understanding and request specific prompts to help it learn, creating a symbiotic relationship between the AI and the prompt engineer.

Ethics and Inclusivity

As we move forward, the importance of ethical and inclusive prompts cannot be understated. There will be an increasing focus on designing prompts that avoid biases and ensure fair and equitable AI responses.

Dynamic Prompt Adjustments

As AI models grow more advanced, we could see dynamic adjustments of prompts based on real-time feedback from AI responses. This would enable the creation of adaptive AI models that learn and improve on the go.

The Shape of Things to Come: More Trends in Prompt Engineering

The trends shaping the world of prompt engineering are as diverse as they are exciting. As we continue our look into the future, here are a few more areas where we can expect to see significant changes and advancements:

Integration with Other AI Fields

As various AI fields evolve, prompt engineering is likely to benefit from these advancements. For instance, reinforcement learning algorithms could be used to optimize the generation of prompts over time. Similarly, advancements in fields like computer vision might make it possible to craft prompts based on visual inputs.

Continual Learning Models

Instead of training AI models in a one-and-done manner, we're moving towards AI that learns continuously from its interactions. In this context, prompt engineering will be crucial for guiding the AI's learning process and ensuring that it evolves in the right direction.

Crowdsourced Prompt Creation

The community's input can be instrumental in creating a broad and diverse set of prompts. We can expect platforms that facilitate the crowdsourcing of prompts, where users can suggest, vote on, and refine prompts.

Regulatory Impact

As AI becomes increasingly integral to our lives, regulatory bodies are likely to play a bigger role in shaping its development. This could influence prompt engineering, with potential guidelines or standards being introduced to ensure the ethical and unbiased use of AI.

More Human-like Interaction

As language models improve, we're moving towards more natural, human-like interactions with AI. Prompts will be crafted not just for functionality, but also to imbue AI with a sense of personality and relatability.

Interdisciplinary Approach

Prompt engineering will increasingly draw upon various fields such as linguistics, psychology, and sociology to understand how to craft effective prompts. This interdisciplinary approach will help us create prompts that are sensitive to cultural nuances, language subtleties, and human emotions.

As we step into this uncharted territory, the only certainty is that exciting times lie ahead. The future will bring challenges, no doubt, but it also holds immense potential. As prompt engineers, we'll need to continually learn, adapt, and innovate to stay on the cutting edge. Here's to boldly explore this next frontier together!

Beyond The Horizon: Further Trends In Prompt Engineering

As we push further into the frontier of prompt engineering, we can see that the opportunities are as vast as the challenges. Here are a few more trends that could shape the future of this exciting field.

Intelligent Tutoring Systems

The education sector could benefit hugely from AI. Expect to see an uptick in prompts that cater to a learner's unique pace and style, making learning more personalized and effective.

Real-Time Prompt Modification

As AI grows faster and more adaptable, we could see the rise of systems that modify prompts in real-time based on user reactions or the unfolding context. This dynamic approach would make AI interactions more responsive and engaging.

The emergence of Standardized Frameworks

As the field matures, we might see the development of standardized frameworks for prompt engineering, making it easier for newcomers to learn the ropes and contribute effectively.

Meta-Learning

Meta-learning, or 'learning to learn,' could become an important part of AI models. Prompt engineers might then have to design meta-prompts that guide not just what the AI learns, but how it learns.

Cross-Lingual Prompts

As AI becomes more global, there will be a need for prompts that work effectively across different languages. This could involve creating prompts in one language and having AI generate responses in another.

Democratization of AI

As AI tools become more user-friendly and accessible, more people will be able to craft their own prompts. This could lead to a much more diverse and creative range of AI applications.

Emotionally Aware Prompts

As AI grows more sophisticated, we could see the emergence of prompts that are designed to elicit and respond to human emotions. This could lead to more empathetic and engaging AI interactions.

Context-Aware Prompts

Future AI models may be better able to understand the context in which a conversation is taking place. This would require designing prompts that can leverage this contextual understanding to generate more relevant and insightful responses.

Specialized Prompt Engineers

As the field matures, we may see more specialization among prompt engineers. Some might focus on crafting prompts for specific industries or applications, while others could specialize in ethical issues or cross-lingual prompts.

Co-creation with AI

Future AI models might be more involved in the prompt engineering process, suggesting modifications to prompts or even creating new ones based on their learning.

Interactive Storytelling

As AI becomes better at understanding and generating human language, we could see a boom in interactive storytelling, where the story evolves based on the reader's inputs. Prompt engineers would play a crucial role in this.

Prompts for AI Ethics

With the growing focus on AI ethics, we might see a rise in prompts designed to train AI models on ethical considerations, helping them navigate complex moral dilemmas.

Remember, the future is not set in stone. It's a world of possibilities that we, as prompt engineers, have the privilege of shaping. So let's embrace these trends and continue pushing the boundaries of what's possible!

Playing Fair: Ethical Considerations In Prompt Engineering

Ah, the twisty, winding path of ethics - it's a journey that requires as much navigation as a trek through the Amazon rainforest, and in the realm of prompt engineering, it's equally as important!

Let's start with an undeniable fact. AI language models, like the ones we're training, are incredibly powerful. They can answer questions, write essays, create poetry, and even crack jokes. However, with great power comes great responsibility. As Spider-Man's Uncle Ben so wisely said, we must ensure we're using this power ethically.

Firstly, it's essential to remember that AI language models learn from vast amounts of text data. Some of this data may be biased, outdated, or offensive. Thus, the models may inadvertently learn and replicate these biases. This is where we, as prompt engineers, need to step in. Our job is not only to create prompts that yield useful responses but also to ensure that these responses are fair, respectful, and unbiased.

To help with this, we can use techniques like bias detection and mitigation during the training process. We can also create prompts that encourage the AI to think critically, question assumptions, and avoid stereotypes. It's a bit like teaching a child to be a good citizen of the world!

Next, we must consider privacy. When using AI, it's crucial to respect the privacy of the users and ensure the model doesn't generate sensitive or personal information. This can be a tricky balance to strike, but it's essential for maintaining trust and promoting the ethical use of AI.

Lastly, there's the issue of consent. When using AI to interact with people, we must ensure that they're aware of it and have given their permission. This is especially important when using AI in public or professional settings.

In the end, ethical prompt engineering is all about putting people first. It's about crafting prompts that respect users' rights and dignity and making sure that our AI partners are behaving appropriately. It's a significant responsibility, but also an incredible opportunity to shape the future of AI in a positive, ethical way. So grab your moral compass, and let's set off on this ethical adventure!

Navigating Legal And Ethical Dilemmas: Ai, Training Data, And Privacy

Treading the path of AI language model training is like a walk on a tightrope, where balance is key, especially when it comes to using people's information, writings, pictures, and other data for training purposes. Several legal and ethical questions pop up in this scenario that we, as prompt engineers, should be well-versed in.

First, there's the question of privacy. The information we use to train AI can come from various sources, like online articles, social media posts, or customer feedback. However, if we use data that includes personal details without explicit consent, we risk breaching privacy rules and regulations. This can lead to legal consequences and damage trust with users.

Second, we have the issue of intellectual property rights. Using someone's writings, images, or any other form of creative expression for training AI without their permission can violate copyright laws. It's essential to ensure that the data used for training is either publicly available and copyright-free or has been explicitly permitted for such use.

Thirdly, there's the matter of informed consent. Even if the data is publicly available, ethical considerations dictate that the data subjects should be aware of and consent to their data being used for AI training. This can be complicated when dealing with large-scale data collection, but transparency and respect for user autonomy are paramount.

Finally, there's the issue of bias. AI language models learn from the data they're trained on. If the training data includes biased information or lacks diversity, the AI can unwittingly perpetuate those biases. Ensuring the data used for training is representative and balanced is a significant ethical challenge.

To navigate these dilemmas, organizations are increasingly developing AI ethics guidelines and adopting Privacy Enhancing Technologies (PETs) to protect user data. There's also a growing emphasis on "privacy by design," where privacy considerations are built into AI systems from the outset.

As prompt engineers, it's our responsibility to understand these legal and ethical nuances and guide our AI training practices accordingly. It's a challenging path, but one that leads to a future where AI is as respectful and fair as it is powerful.

Your Journey Ahead: Preparing For A Career In Prompt Engineering

You are standing at the threshold of a field that is at once a science and an art. On one hand, it requires a deep understanding of artificial intelligence, natural language processing, machine learning, and data analysis - hard skills that are crucial in today's tech-driven world. On the other hand, it requires creativity, empathy, and a flair for communication - soft skills that bring the 'human touch' to the algorithms and data.

As a prompt engineer, you are not just a coder or a data analyst. You are a bridge between human language and machine intelligence. You are a magician who commands the AI with your prompts, a craftsman who fine-tunes its responses, and a guardian who ensures its power is used ethically and responsibly.

So how do you prepare for this exciting career? Firstly, you need to arm yourself with knowledge. Read widely about AI and machine learning. Familiarize yourself with Python, the language of choice for most AI applications. Learn about natural language processing, the technology that enables machines to understand and generate human language.

But don't stop at technical skills. Hone your communication skills as well. Learn how to craft clear, effective prompts. Develop an understanding of human psychology, so you can anticipate how users might interact with the AI. Practice critical thinking and problem-solving, so you can navigate the challenges that will inevitably arise.

Next, get hands-on experience. Look for opportunities to work on AI projects, whether it's through your job, internships, or personal projects. Experiment with different prompts, observe how the AI responds, and learn from your successes and failures.

Don't forget to keep an eye on the future. Stay abreast of the latest trends in AI and prompt engineering. Attend seminars, webinars, and conferences. Join online forums and communities. Be a lifelong learner, always ready to adapt and evolve.

The world of AI and language models is evolving at a rapid pace. Stay curious, keep asking questions, and constantly seek to improve your understanding. Explore new techniques, technologies, and trends. Innovation is driven by curiosity.

The best ideas often come from collaboration. Join communities of AI enthusiasts, participate in online forums, and attend industry events. Networking with peers can provide opportunities to learn from other's experiences and perspectives.

As with any technical field, you'll encounter challenges and setbacks. A model might not understand a prompt as you'd expect, or you might struggle to fine-tune a response. It's important to remain patient, keep trying different approaches, and learn from these experiences.

As a prompt engineer, you're a gatekeeper for responsible AI usage. You have to ensure that the AI operates within ethical boundaries and respects users' privacy. Study the ethical considerations in AI and make them a key part of your practice.

As a bridge between the technical world of AI and the users who interact with it, clear communication is essential. You have to understand the technology and be able to explain it to non-technical people. Work on translating complex ideas into understandable concepts.

Always keep the end user in mind. Understanding the user's needs, expectations, and context can help you craft better prompts and design better interactions with the AI.

Depending on your background, consider pursuing further education in AI or related fields, such as data science, computer science, or statistics. There are many online courses, boot camps, and certification programs that can provide you with the specialized knowledge you need to understand and work with AI systems.

Practical experience is often just as important as formal education in the tech industry. Consider working on your own AI projects to gain hands-on experience and showcase your skills. You can include these projects in your portfolio, which you can then present to potential employers.

This is an excellent way to gain real-world experience and learn from others in the field. It also shows potential employers that you're actively engaged in learning and contributing to the AI community.

Attend AI-focused meetups, workshops, webinars, and conferences to meet professionals in the field. Networking can often lead to job opportunities. Also, join AI-related groups on LinkedIn and other social media platforms to stay up-to-date on industry trends and job openings.

Use job search platforms to find AI-related job openings. Make sure your resume and LinkedIn profile highlight your AI-related skills, projects, and any other relevant experience.

Understanding the industry in which you plan to apply your AI skills can be as important as understanding AI itself. If you're interested in healthcare, for example, having knowledge about healthcare systems, regulations, and data privacy concerns can be a major asset.

AI is a rapidly evolving field, and continuous learning is a must to stay current. This could mean regularly taking new courses, reading up on the latest research, or experimenting with the latest AI software and tools. Continue to learn and upskill, whether it's through formal education, online courses, or self-study.

Remember, your journey as a prompt engineer is not a sprint but a marathon. It's a journey of continuous learning and growth, filled with both challenges and triumphs. But with determination, curiosity, and a sense of adventure, you are sure to succeed. Lastly, remember that every path is unique, and there's no one-size-fits-all approach to starting a career in AI. Follow your interests, continue to learn and grow, and seize opportunities as they arise. Good luck!

BEYOND THE WEB INTERFACE: DIVERSE APPLICATIONS OF PROMPTS

Now that we've traversed through the intricate maze of prompt engineering, mastered its craft, unearthed its secrets, and peeked into its future, it's time to step out and look at the bigger picture.

Beyond the web interface, the applications of prompt engineering are as diverse as the imagination allows. In this technology-driven world where AI models are becoming increasingly embedded in our everyday lives, prompt engineering becomes an essential component not just behind the screens, but in shaping our digital future.

In this chapter, we'll dive into how prompts are utilized in various contexts, from speech to text, text to speech, document handling, data extraction, and even extending to the broader horizons of IoT devices and applications. Whether it's your smartphone assistant understanding your spoken requests, or your email client suggesting the perfect reply, or an intelligent system parsing complex documents, prompts are working diligently behind the scenes.

As we explore these diverse applications, we'll see how they require distinct considerations and techniques, amplifying the significance of expertly crafted prompts. These scenarios provide opportunities to apply what we've learned in new and fascinating ways, truly bringing prompt engineering to life.

Prompts In Email Communication

Emails! Love them or hate them, they're a ubiquitous part of our digital lives. And with the advent of AI, they've gotten a whole lot smarter. Welcome to the realm of email communication, where prompts are used to turn those monotonous mail-merging tasks into an AI-powered breeze.

Have you ever noticed how some email clients can offer suggestions to finish your sentences or even auto-generate short replies? Those are the result of expertly designed prompts working with sophisticated language models.

But how does it happen? Well, when you start writing an email, the AI is given a prompt in the form of the text you've already written. Then, the language model uses this prompt to generate a range of potential completions, whether it's finishing a sentence or suggesting a complete reply. This process saves time, reduces cognitive load, and helps maintain a professional tone, especially handy when you're dealing with a full inbox.

But it's not just about crafting sentences. Prompts also come into play for more complex tasks like organizing your emails. For instance, AI can be used to categorize your emails based on their content, send automatic replies based on specific triggers, or even summarize the key points from lengthy threads.

It's important to note that prompt engineering in the context of email communication requires a good understanding of the subtleties of language and the etiquette of professional communication. Also, since we're dealing with potentially sensitive data, there are serious considerations regarding privacy and data security.

In essence, prompts help in creating smarter, more efficient, and highly personalized email experiences. It's a testament to the power of prompt engineering and an exciting glimpse into how AI is transforming our everyday digital interactions. Let's continue our journey to uncover how prompts are making waves in other fields.

Voice-Activated Systems: Speech-To-Text

Enter the realm of voice-activated systems - a domain where prompt engineering and technology combine to translate human speech into written text. From dictation tools and voice assistants to transcription services and more, this is where we truly witness the magic of language models in action.

Imagine this: You're driving to work, and an important thought about a project pops into your head. With a simple voice command to your digital assistant, you're able to draft an email without taking your hands off the wheel. That's the power of a well-crafted prompt functioning in a speech-to-text system!

These systems utilize a combination of speech recognition and natural language processing to interpret human language and translate it into written form. The prompts play a crucial role in guiding the AI to understand the context, purpose, and desired format of the user's request.

Creating prompts for voice-activated systems poses unique challenges and requires a careful consideration of the elements of human speech. People often use informal, incomplete, or grammatically incorrect sentences when speaking, especially to AI systems. They also include a lot of fillers like "um" and "uh." In such scenarios, the AI needs to be trained to disregard these irrelevant parts and focus on the essential elements that need to be transcribed or actioned upon. This underlines the importance of crafting flexible and forgiving prompts that can handle a wide range of speech patterns and accents.

Moreover, these systems often require real-time processing, adding another layer of complexity to prompt design. They also involve an array of privacy and accessibility considerations that need to be accounted for.

Unfolding the potential of speech-to-text systems is like opening a box full of opportunities. They're revolutionizing many sectors, including healthcare, customer service, legal services, and more. As we learn to engineer more precise and efficient prompts, we're inching closer to breaking down the barriers between humans and machines, one voice command at a time. Now, let's move on to see how prompts breathe life into text-to-speech systems.

Text-To-Speech Systems

From audiobooks to voice assistants, text-to-speech (TTS) systems are a marvel that has brought about a significant transformation in the way we interact with technology. Imagine being able to have any piece of text read out to you, whether it's the morning news, your favourite book, or crucial business documents. Sounds futuristic, right? But that's the power of text-to-speech systems, and prompts are at the heart of this technology!

In a TTS system, the input is a piece of text, and the output is an audio recording of that text being spoken. Prompts come into play as instructions that guide the AI to generate an appropriate speech response. They determine the tone, pace, pitch, and other characteristics of the generated speech, making the output sound more human-like.

Crafting prompts for TTS systems requires a solid understanding of both language and sound. For example, consider the difference between a statement and a question, or a command and a request. The punctuation and wording in the text provide cues about how the speech should sound, and the prompt needs to encapsulate these nuances.

Moreover, language models used in TTS systems need to handle a wide range of texts, from simple sentences to complex paragraphs. And it's not just about reading the text verbatim. Depending on the application, the system might need to summarize, translate, or interpret the text in some way before speaking it out.

As an AI prompt engineer, creating prompts for TTS systems can be an interesting challenge. You're essentially teaching a machine how to talk in a way that sounds natural and easy to understand. The possibilities are immense, and the potential to improve accessibility and convenience is even more significant.

As we dive deeper into this exciting realm, it's evident that prompt engineering is much more than creating text instructions. It's about envisioning the future of human-machine interactions and playing a pivotal role in shaping it.

Ai Chatbots And Customer Service

Stepping into the realm of AI chatbots and customer service, we find ourselves at the bustling intersection of technology and business. Chatbots have revolutionized customer service, replacing long waiting times and limited support hours with instantaneous, round-the-clock assistance. And guess what's powering these chatbots to understand and respond to customer queries? You guessed it, it's our superhero - well-crafted prompts!

From answering frequently asked questions and providing product information to resolving complaints and even upselling, AI chatbots are transforming customer interactions. As a prompt engineer, you're tasked with the job of ensuring these AI-powered virtual assistants respond accurately and engagingly to customers' needs.

You see, unlike traditional software, chatbots don't rely on pre-defined responses. They use AI and language models to understand user inputs and generate appropriate replies. This is where the magic of prompt engineering comes in. A well-structured prompt can guide the chatbot to understand the customer's intent and deliver a meaningful response. For instance, a prompt can help distinguish whether a customer is inquiring about a new product, complaining about an existing one, or seeking help with a technical issue.

Crafting prompts for AI chatbots involves a good understanding of both technology and the unique characteristics of customer service communication. It requires empathy, insight into customer needs, and the ability to envision various customer interaction scenarios.

Consider the complexity of language and the wide range of expressions customers use. Then add the need for the chatbot to maintain a professional and helpful tone, and you begin to grasp the challenges and complexity of this domain.

Moreover, with the increasing need for personalized and intuitive customer experiences, the demand for skilled prompt engineers in this field is growing.

Next, we'll take a look at the role of prompts in extracting data from documents.

Automated Document Generation

Let's dive into an area of prompt engineering that is a life-saver for many industries: automated document generation. Ever wished you could click a button and have a polished, fully formed document spit out in seconds? Well, in the world of AI, you can do just that. Here, prompts play a crucial role in instructing the AI on the kind of document to produce.

Think about a company that needs to generate monthly reports. Rather than having an employee dedicate time and effort to manually compile these reports, you could have an AI model generate them at the drop of a hat. All you need to do is to provide the right prompts. You feed the model relevant data and a series of instructions - the prompts.

The prompts act as a guide for the AI to interpret and structure the data into the desired format. For instance, your prompts could instruct the AI to compile sales figures, identify the best-performing products, and highlight significant changes from the previous month, all while maintaining a professional tone. With the right prompts, the AI can generate a comprehensive, ready-to-present report with all the necessary insights, saving precious time and resources.

Now imagine applying this to an array of documents - from proposals and contracts to emails and blog posts. The possibilities are endless, and they're all within your reach as a prompt engineer.

The challenge is in creating prompts that effectively translate the desired output into commands that the AI can understand. This requires not just a thorough understanding of the AI language model you're working with, but also a dash of creativity and a whole lot of empathy. You're bridging the gap between human needs and AI capabilities, and that's where the magic happens.

As we journey further into the different applications of prompt engineering, remember this: you're not just a coder or a data analyst. You're an artist, a linguist, a psychologist, and a problem solver. You're a prompt engineer.

Search Engines

Every time you've typed a question into Google, hit 'Enter', and been presented with a perfectly fitting answer or a page of search results that hit the mark, you've interacted with the power of prompts in search engines. It's the understated art of turning your query into a journey through the vast information network that is the internet.

Search engines use sophisticated AI systems, and they rely heavily on prompts to parse through millions of possible data points to find what's most relevant for you. They have to understand the query, and the intent behind it, and then deliver the most appropriate response. In essence, every search query is a prompt, guiding the AI system to produce the required output.

As a prompt engineer, you'll be the maestro of this interaction, orchestrating the way AI systems interpret and respond to search queries. Say someone searches for "best pizza places in New York." This isn't just a random string of words. It's a prompt asking the AI to find highly-rated pizza restaurants in a specific geographical location.

But prompt engineering isn't just about understanding queries. It's also about enhancing AI's ability to provide more relevant results. For instance, understanding that a search for "Why is my plant wilting?" requires resources on plant care rather than botanical scientific papers. The AI needs to differentiate between different user requirements, and prompts are a key tool to guide this process.

Mastering this aspect of prompt engineering involves a deep understanding of language, context, and user intent, creating a seamless user experience that feels almost magical. In the ever-evolving landscape of AI and search, it's an exciting and continually challenging field.

Social Media

When it comes to crafting a personalized user experience, few arenas are as dynamic and demanding as social media. From Facebook and Instagram to Twitter and TikTok, each platform serves up a custom-curated stream of content tailored to the individual's preferences, interactions, and behaviours. Have you ever wondered what powers this personalized content delivery? You guessed it—prompts!

Every like, share, comment, or scroll on a social media platform is a form of prompt. These prompts feed into the underlying AI algorithms that shape your social media experience, teaching them about your interests, preferences, and engagement patterns. As a result, the AI can predict and serve up the kind of content you're most likely to engage with.

As a prompt engineer working with social media platforms, your role involves more than just understanding these prompts. It's about optimizing them, creating effective and engaging prompts that guide the AI in understanding the user better, and crafting a more engaging, personalized experience.

Consider a user who frequently engages with posts about dogs. The AI, prompted by this behaviour, might start showing more dog-related content. But as a prompt engineer, your role is to guide the AI in understanding the nuance of these interactions. Are they interested in adopting a dog? Or perhaps they're interested in dog training techniques? Or maybe they just enjoy humorous dog videos? By fine-tuning the prompts, you can guide the AI to make these distinctions and deliver a more tailored content feed.

Prompts in social media aren't just about enhancing user experience—they also play a crucial role in safety and moderation. They help AI systems identify and respond to harmful content, from spam and scams to hate speech and misinformation. The role of a prompt engineer, therefore, also encompasses creating prompts that promote a safe and positive social media environment.

Education And Online Learning Platforms

In the realm of education, AI has emerged as a powerful tool, personalizing learning experiences and paving the way for the classroom of the future. From language learning apps like Duolingo to comprehensive platforms such as Khan Academy, AI is shaping how we learn—and prompts play a pivotal role in this process.

When you interact with an online learning platform, every question you answer, every topic you click, every video you watch—it all serves as a prompt. These prompts guide the AI in understanding your learning style, your proficiency in different topics, and the areas where you might need more help. As a result, the AI can tailor the learning experience to your individual needs, providing personalized guidance and resources.

As a prompt engineer in the education space, your role is about more than creating effective prompts. It's about shaping the future of learning. Imagine being able to design prompts that can help a struggling student grasp a difficult concept, or that can challenge a high-achieving student to reach new heights. Or consider the power of prompts in helping an AI identify when a student might be dealing with learning difficulties, such as dyslexia, and then adjust its teaching approach accordingly.

Prompts also play a significant role in the evaluation and feedback process in online learning platforms. They guide the AI in assessing student performance, identifying gaps in understanding, and providing constructive feedback. From setting up complex problem-solving scenarios to crafting thoughtful review questions, your work as a prompt engineer can deeply impact the learning outcomes for students around the world.

EMBARKING ON YOUR PROMPT ENGINEERING JOURNEY: NEXT STEPS

As the final chapter of this book unfolds, you're standing at the threshold of an exhilarating journey. Our expedition through the fascinating landscape of prompt engineering may be coming to a close, but for you, an exciting new adventure is just about to begin.

From the first moment, we started to unravel the enigmatic world of AI and Language Models, through our exploration of the indispensable tools and techniques of prompt engineering, to envisioning the boundless possibilities of the future, we have navigated vast and varied terrain. But as with all great adventures, reaching the end of one journey merely heralds the start of another.

We have ventured into the heart of AI systems, breaking down complex concepts into comprehensible nuggets of knowledge. We have journeyed through the daily life of a prompt engineers, revealing the vital role they play in crafting the interactions between humans and AI. We have traversed the intricate pathways of prompt design, understanding how to elicit the desired responses from an AI model. We've also scrutinized the successes and failures of past projects, extracting valuable lessons that will serve as signposts for your journey ahead.

Throughout this process, our guiding beacon has been the belief that anyone armed with curiosity, persistence, and the right knowledge can master the art of prompt engineering. It's about understanding the magic that breathes life into AI language models and using this knowledge to create meaningful, effective interactions between humans and AI.

Yet, the realm of AI is like an endless universe, constantly expanding and evolving. New technologies are being invented, new applications are being discovered, and new challenges are emerging on the horizon. And amidst this continuous flux, the role of the prompt engineer is becoming ever more critical and exciting.

Now, as you stand ready to embark on your own prompt engineering journey, remember that every end is a new beginning. The conclusion of this book doesn't signify the end of your learning. Instead, it marks the start of your exploration, experimentation, and evolution in the real world. So, as we delve into this concluding chapter, let's look forward to the next steps on your exciting journey, and let's celebrate your inauguration into the captivating world of prompt engineering.

Becoming Fluent In The Language Of Ai:

The world of AI is an enthralling symphony of several programming languages, tools, and frameworks. While Python stands out for its simplicity and extensive library support, languages like R, Java, and C++ also find their place in the AI universe. Depending on your interest and the nature of your project, you might need to learn one or more of these languages.

Python: Known for its readability and simplicity, Python is the most widely used language in the AI and Machine Learning community. Libraries such as TensorFlow, PyTorch, and Keras make it a go-to choice for building neural networks. For beginners, Python's easy syntax serves as an excellent springboard into the world of programming. There are numerous resources available to learn Python online, some of which are Codecademy, Coursera, and SoloLearn.

R: If you're more into statistics and data analysis, R is your language. Its powerful packages for statistical analysis, graphics representation, and reporting make it a favourite among statisticians and data scientists.

Java: As one of the oldest programming languages, Java finds its use in building scalable AI applications, especially in big companies.

C++: If performance is your utmost priority, C++ should be your choice. AI applications that are performance-critical (like game playing, robotics, etc.) often prefer C++ over other languages.

Besides these, there are a few other programming languages like Julia, Swift, and Scala, which are also getting traction in the AI community. As a budding prompt engineer, you may want to start with Python due to its ease of learning and extensive support in AI. However, remember that learning a programming language is not an end in itself but a means to an end: to translate your ideas into a language that machines understand. Choose a language that fits best with your interests and career goals.

In the following sections, we'll discuss how you can take your first steps in AI programming and prompt engineering by learning these languages and mastering the tools that will help you bring your AI dreams to life.

The Path To Mastery: Continuous Learning In

Prompt Engineering

The field of AI, particularly prompt engineering, is in a state of constant evolution. Today's innovations might become tomorrow's basic tools, while newer, more advanced techniques continually emerge. The path to mastery in this field, therefore, involves an ongoing commitment to learning and staying informed about the latest developments.

Being part of the AI community is a remarkable way to facilitate this learning process. There are countless online forums, social media groups, and professional networks dedicated to AI and machine learning, where you can participate in stimulating discussions, share ideas, and learn from the experiences of others. Some of these include communities like Stack Overflow, Reddit's Machine Learning subreddit, and GitHub, to name a few.

Attending AI-related workshops, webinars, and conferences also provides an excellent opportunity to get insights into the latest research and developments in the field. These events often feature presentations by experts in the field, providing a wealth of knowledge and an opportunity to ask questions and gain in-depth understanding. Additionally, they often offer hands-on workshops or hackathons, where you can put your skills to the test and learn in a practical, engaging environment.

Another great learning avenue is online courses. Platforms like Coursera, edX, and Udacity offer high-quality AI and machine learning courses, designed and taught by industry and academic experts. These courses often include project-based learning, providing a valuable opportunity to apply what you've learned in a practical context.

Don't forget to get your hands dirty with coding as well! Practical experience is invaluable in prompt engineering. You can start with small projects or participate in coding challenges on platforms like Kaggle or Codewars. As you gain confidence, you can work on more complex projects, gradually honing your skills and understanding.

Remember, the path to mastery in prompt engineering isn't a sprint; it's a marathon. Patience, persistence, and an insatiable curiosity to learn are your best companions on this exciting journey. And while it may seem daunting at first, remember that every expert was once a beginner. So, stay positive, keep learning, and most importantly, have fun on this incredible journey of discovery and innovation.

CONCLUSION: EMBRACING
THE LOOM OF THE FUTURE

I n the early part of the 19th century, an unprecedented technological shift forever changed the landscape of textile manufacturing. Lace makers, whose meticulous handiwork had been the cornerstone of the industry, found their roles drastically altered with the advent of automated lace looms. While some feared the obsolescence of their craft, the changes brought on new roles and challenges that required human ingenuity, craftsmanship, and oversight as much as before, if not more.

In many ways, the age of AI and prompt engineering parallels this historic shift. The introduction of AI and language models into our everyday lives is a tectonic shift that promises to revolutionize the way we work, communicate, and engage with the world around us. Just as the lace loom wasn't the end of craftsmanship but rather an evolution, the advent of AI doesn't signify an end to human ingenuity, but a metamorphosis into something more powerful and expansive.

As we stand at this crossroads, the future may seem daunting. But history has shown us that such pivotal moments are not only a challenge but an opportunity. The role of prompt engineers, akin to the lace makers adapting to the mechanical loom, is to guide this technological transformation, shape its development, and ensure its responsible use.

As we move forward, we must embrace the loom of our future, AI, and harness its power to enhance our work, improve our communications, and enrich our lives. The era of AI is not one to fear but one to seize with both hands and as budding prompt engineers, you are in the driver's seat.

In the chapters of this book, we have explored the art and science of prompt engineering, its potential, its challenges, and the fascinating prospects it holds for the future. We hope that this journey has been enlightening and invigorating. As you step into the world of prompt engineering, remember, each prompt you craft is a stitch in the fabric of this evolving AI narrative.

Welcome to the future